Buffalo and Cattle Refuges

Maybe you hated watching Buffalo play in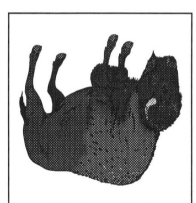
the Super
Bowl, but
you'll love
them at the
National
Wildlife
Reserve. And
if buffalo don't
do it for you,
then there are
plenty of
Texas
longhorn cattle, as well as deer and elk
who will gladly pose for pictures.

Wichita Mountains in Oklahoma and Fort
Niobrara in Nebraska preserve these
animals in their natural habitat. For more
information, contact Fort Niobrara National
Wildlife Refuge, Hidden Timber Route, HC
14, Box 67, Valentine, NE 69201; or
402-376-3789. Wichita Mountains Wildlife
Refuge, Rt. 1, Box 448, Indiahoma, OK
73552; 405-429-3221. Another resource is
National Bison Range, Moise, MT 59824;
406-644-2211.

Hotline to 10,000 "Rooms"

Maybe you don't need marble bathrooms or a king-size bed, or even room service for you to call it a vacation. All you need is a place to pull in for the night.

You can call all the Forest Service toll-free hotline to make a reservation at one of the 156 National Forests, where you can hike, fish, camp, ski, or just relax on over 100,000 miles of trails and 10,000 recreation sites. Call the toll-free number to make reservations for any of the National Forests at 800-238-CAMP.

☆ ☆ ☆

Have Them Pay Your Ticket

Did you know that the government will pay you $50 a day to teach kids in Tanzania to throw a shot putt, or $100 a day to talk about women's rights in Bangladesh? And that includes round-trip airfare.

If you have had a unique American experience or hold a particular expertise, you can join the likes of Sandra Day O'Connor, Sally Ride, and John Updike who are just a few of those who have

HE
WALKED THE
AMERICAS

L. TAYLOR HANSEN

LEGEND PRESS
Amherst, Wisconsin

Twenty-second Printing, 2003
Copyright© 1963 by L. Taylor Hansen
Copyright© renewed 1991

Published by
Ray Palmer
LEGEND PRESS
9533 Clinton Road
Amherst, WI 54406
lgpress@hotmail.com
Printed in Hong Kong

ISBN 0-9644997-0-3

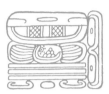

To Elaine Beam one whose warm friendship and understanding has followed the author and the building of this book legend by legend through study, interview and travel for over thirty years, and whose love of the search is in every way equal to my own.

And to Lord Kingsborough who gave his fortune and finally his life to the Legend, as he died in a debtor's prison.

Also to the brave medicine man of the Seri who was blinded for telling the legend of The Healer without the permission of the tribe.

Contents

Illustrations

Acknowledgements

THE AUTHOR wishes to express profound gratitude to Dr. Robert E. Bell, anthropologist of Oklahoma University and world authority on the Spiro Mound and its excavation. Not only did this busy scientist take hours of his precious time searching the files for the present location of the shards showing winged-beings and the hand with the cross through the centre, but he also suggested numerous pamphlets for further study and gave help on the subject of carbon-dating.

Nor can I send this book to press without mentioning Dr. Clarke Wissler. Although Curator of the Heye Foundation for the American Indian Museum for most of his lifetime, this world-famous anthropologist spent hours writing letters suggesting where old volumes might be found; what tribes to contact for further study of the Prophet Legend; where the oldest Mounds still extant might be located, and what Indian leaders might be induced to talk. This contact with the author continued to the time of his death. As his friends among the Red Men would say: May he walk in beauty forever through the Land of Shadows.

And lastly, my thanks to the National Railways of Mexico for their courtesy in permitting reproduction of photographs owned by them.

Introduction

THESE ARE THE legends of The Healer. This is the drama of Mahnt-Azoma, or Tl-Acoma, The Mighty, sometimes called Kate-Zahl, The Prophet. The backdrop is not the land as we know it, for the action moves through many climates changed by the passage of two millenia; through mines long buried under a forest cover; through valleys once fertile and rich in commerce which have long returned to barren desert; down highways now covered by the strangling jungle or lost in the silt of other ages; through cities whose legendary beauty is still whispered by the story tellers of a hundred nations.

The sequence of these fire-light legends, particularly vivid among the wild tribes, form one by one a curious pattern. It is the story of a saintly white teacher, whose hands performed miracles of healing, and whose strange eyes, grey-green as the ocean, looked down the vistas of the future.

His symbol is woven into blankets; carved upon the walls of canyons; burned into pottery; danced in dances. His name is given to rushing rivers; tall white mountains; sacred forests; springs of never ending water.

Strong is this tale of the Ancient Americas, but broken like a chain of gems long-scattered. Running it backward, as one must to find the beginning, the seeker finds himself in Pacha-ca-mac, once queen of the Peruvian shoreline, now long returned to rubble and ruin. Here He stares across the wide Pacific - for it was from thence He came; He who always asked the people to name Him, and one of whose names, among many others was The Lord-Of-Wind-And-Water, Tah-co-mah or Kate-Zahl, The Prophet.

All the glory of the Godhead
   Had the Prophet, Quetzal-Coatl;
All the honor of the people,
   Sanctified his name, and holy;
And their prayers they offered to him
   In the days of ancient Tula.

*Translated from the Aztec
by Dr. Corwyn of Mexico University.*

F. Catherwood.

Figure in bas-relief on stone on one of the jambs of the Teocallis at Chichen Itza.

A Reminder From The Ancients
Of The Broad Land

"WE ARE The Ancients, and our skin is red: with us, the Sacred Color. These are our legends told about the campfires on winter's evenings. When you string them together, remember our great pride. Now we are looking down and our feathers are drooping. Tell the legends so that our young men will realize that the ancestor threads run in many directions. Through the tribes we have captured and with whom we have intermarried there is a red thread which runs back to the Red Land long sunken in the Destruction. There is a thread which runs far to the south where the mountain tops touch the sky and the Thunder Bird moves through the lightnings. There is a golden thread which touches Tollan, The Mighty, and beautiful Tula, while through some of our mothers there is a white thread to the words of The Prophet. Tell my young men to listen." - Asa Delugie, War Chief of The Mescallero Apaches.

"This is our book. May you write it in beauty as we have told it in beauty." - Zeahley Tso, Chief of The Navaho.

"There is evidence that some of our ancestors may have come from the ancient trading empire of ChanChan centuries before the rise of the Incan Power in Peru. Tell my people to learn of this great power which once ruled eyes. Tell them to look up and learn." - So-Sah-kuku, Chief Snake Priest of Oraibi.

"This is our book - these legends of Ancient times. They are of the blood which courses through our veins. We of the Seven Tribes of the Black Tortoise once had a Dream of Empire. Yet farther back through the cycles of Time we knew the Great Wakon-Tah, but we forgot His words. These legends should help us to look up and remember. - Shooting-Star, of the Hunkapa Dacotah.

13

The God Wakea

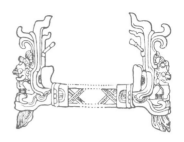

ONCE IN THE days long-vanished, with three great ships which had sailed from the Sunset-lands, came white-robed Wakea - the Fair God who healed the injured, raised the dead, and walked on water. He came to an out-lying island of the Tahitian group where two tribes were fighting bitterly.

Now, however, the Polynesians are all one people, anciently calling themselves Maori, from New Zealand to Easter Island off the South American coastline. They were the vikings of the sunrise, rowing their long-boats over the trackless ocean, guiding themselves by the stars of the heavens, and speaking one language from Hawaii southward. They used the same plants, kept the same animals and sang the same songs of the ancients. One of these was of the god Wakea.

To an island where men were fighting for the possession of the good land came three ships with giant sails like enormous birds with wings up-lifted, glowing goldenly in the dawn-light. Suddenly frozen to immobility were the warriors as the ships moved around a jutting headland.

"What manner of monsters are these with the great wings?"

"Perhaps they have come to devour the people!"

Forgotten was the heat of the battle. Friend and foe stood facing seaward, weapons clutched in paralyzed fingers, staring in wide-eyed wonder.

The ships' oarsmen, whose paddles looked like a hundred centipede legs touching the water, rested now from their task of moving the giant monsters forward.

Then the islanders saw something white moving toward

Sandwich Islanders.

them. Apparently it had come from the Great Birds, and it glided easily over the water with the rhythmical ease of a man walking.

As the spot of white came closer, they saw in amazement that this was a Fair God, man-like in form, but unlike their people. Soon they could see Him clearly, the gold of the dawn-light shining behind and around Him, making a halo of His long-curling hair and beard. They saw the foam-like swish of His garments. As He came up on the wet sand, the warriors stared in fright at His garments; they were dry. Now they knew that a god stood among them, for none but gods can walk on water!

From His garments, so foam-white, they looked to His pale face and then into His eyes. They were strange eyes, grey-green as the depths of the water, and like it, ever changing. Now those eyes flashed with anger as He stared about him and looked upon the injured.

A god had come from the sea to walk among them and His first look was that of anger! The warriors fell down as one man and began an old chant anciently employed to a

Breadfruit tree.

god for forgiveness. When they dared again to raise up their own eyes, they saw Him going among the injured and dying who arose from their pain to find themselves well of body as soon as His hand or His garments had touched them.

Thus on this never to be forgotten day came the beloved Wakea to live for awhile among the people.

When the villagers arrived with presents, creeping on their knees toward Him, He signaled the ships. Small boats now left the Great Birds and brought other strangers. These men, though something like him in features, and like Him bearded, were different in two ways from the god

Wakea. Most plain to see was that their garments were not white, but colored. But there was something beside this material difference: it was the way these friends looked upon their leader. In their eyes one could see their reverence. In their strange speech one could feel their great love.

Friend and foe among the Polynesians now set about to entertain the strangers. Putting forth their choicest dishes, making welcome with song and dances, they invited the strangers to partake of the great feast. They had planned an entire night of merry-making, but alas, as the sun began to paint the western sky with the colors of the orchids, hanging in profusion in the forest, they could see that the strangers were preparing to leave them.

The sadness they had felt at this discovery was suddenly reversed when they saw the strangers bidding tearful farewell to the god Wakea. Scarcely had the people dreamed of this good fortune, for now it was becoming very

Maori Prince's staffs and baton.

obvious that the god Wakea was planning no journey, but would remain among them.

Respectfully at a short distance stood the people, while Wakea comforted the tearful strangers. They saw Him point to the direction of the sunrise, and wondered among themselves what He might be saying in His strange language.

Then, after many further embraces, they watched the strangers enter the small boats and row back to the great bird-ships. As Wakea stood there on the sand watching sadly, the chief stepped up quietly and pointed to a high point which looked over the jutting headland around which the ships were now passing. Wakea nodded quickly, followed the Chief and some of the people to the sun-painted high point. There they together watched the three ships move into the sunset, fading at last into the sea of beauty. Only then did they return to the village, and the great ships were nevermore seen by the tribesmen.

Very quickly Wakea learned Polynesian. The people were amazed at the speed of his learning. As the long days passed, He began to teach the tribesmen. He told them of the One God who ruled the Heavens, who spoke through the volcanoes and who breathed on the ocean. To Him, war was not of His making, for His law was Love One Another. For Wakea they gave up war and the sacrifice of children which had kept down their populations so they would not overeat their islands.

Then the men carried Him with them, taking Wakea from island to island so each one would meet the strange Fair God whose hands were miracles of healing. Many then were the songs of Wakea and many the legends, which down the long vistas of time have been forgotten. Yet His name has been never forgotten.

Ship carved in stone on wall at Chichen Itza.

Wakea had one strange custom. Every morning before dawn He would rise and pray toward the dawn-star on some high point facing seaward. When they asked Him why He did this He said that even so would His friends be praying in

Maori chieftains.

that far-off land across the ocean.

The people remembered, thought of that day when He had come to them; of His friends who had wept when they were leaving; and how He had pointed for them toward the sunrise heavens.

Finally the Fair God knew well all of the islands, and there was not one where He had not landed, feasted with and taught the people. It was then that He looked more often toward the direction of the dawning, and asked questions about the Lands Of The Dawn Star. The people were not entirely unacquainted with the continent lying eastward. Did they not have the yam to eat, and call it by its ancient South American name? Yet they were loathe to lose the Healer, this strange god who answered to the name they had given him: Wakea, the Fair God Of The Ocean.

As long as they could, they tried to dissuade His growing wish to travel eastward. Yet they loved Him too much to deny His desire, and so preparations were made for the long journey to be made in the Boats Of The Migrations.

Through their tears the people watched Him take His seat in the long boat while one child called out in a voice broken by sobbing:

"Are we never again to see you Wakea?"

In His melodious voice the Fair God made answer:

"One day you will see me returning, even as I came, through the light of the dawning, if you remember to keep my commandments and always love one another."

The canoes of many rowers carried much food and water. Through wind and storm they stayed together, keeping each other in sight in the day time, and at night by alternate chanting.

Thus from the islands and into the sunrise, rode the Long Boats carrying Wakea, beautiful creature of peace and laughter whose curling brown hair trapped the red-gold of sunlight and whose strange level eyes held the sea's deepest mystery, changing like the water in light and shadow.

So the Fair God moved into the dawn toward the Lands Of The Dawn Star, sped onward by the chants of farewell sung by the sorrowing people. And since that day, though some have said that He is sometimes seen in spirit, yet in the flesh they are still waiting for Him to come back to His beloved islands of Polynesia.

(Author's note: To Dr. Buck, who wrote "Vikings of The Sunrise", and beside being himself a Polynesian was a scholar of the past of his people, we owe the answers to the following questions, put to him in a personal letter:

"Do you know of a prophet or teacher who came among the Polynesian Islands, teaching theology and agriculture? He dressed in a long white toga-like garment. His eyes were grey-green, his long light brown hair had reddish highlights, and he was bearded. If you recognize this figure, please tell me his name, his century, and the manner of his coming. From which direction did he arrive, and whence take his departure? That is, if your legends can answer these questions."

20

An answer came both briefly and formally from the Bishop Museum where he was the Director.

"I recognize this figure from our legends. His name is Wakea. The other questions I cannot answer, much as they intrigue me. However, I am to go to an outlying island of the Tahitians where two old women can still chant the ancestor-legends. From them, and another in a different island, I hope to learn the answers. Therefore, in two or three months you will hear from me again."

In three months, as promised, came the second letter.

"Wakea, the Healer, lived in the first century of the Christian Era, or generally speaking, in the time of Jesus.

"It seems that He came in the early dawning of our history to these tribes who were fighting in this outlying island. I am enclosing a copy of the story as it was told to me.")

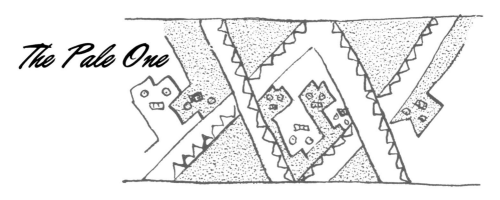

The Pale One

Nasca cat-face design.

IN THE CITY of ancient glory, Pachacamac, queen of the ocean, high upon the glittering temple built they tell you to the Fish God, stood He who was called Wakea by some, and by others Wako.

His temple, built by the wealth of the ages, dated back so far into forgotten time that men no longer remembered its building. Now the long rays of the morning sunlight caught it up in dazzling splendor, lit its tiers of jet, high-polished alternated with crested goldwork, rising above the quiet city like a glorious pyramid-mountain.

Upon the summit stood The Pale One, beard and hair and robe gold-tinted, as was the incense which swirled above Him with its scent of burning cedar.

Far below in the agate courtyard, mosaiced in designs of eternal beauty, the people danced in ceremony, ancient steps of intricate rhythm telling of their deep devotion.

Beyond the courtyard stretched the city. The sun rays lit its whitewashed houses, its orchards, markets, parks and causeways reaching beyond the outmost dwelling in straight, wide paved highways running to the four directions. At the docks were the ships of the traders, the long balsa ships which carried their pottery to Oaxaca and other ports far-distant, and traded their yams to the Maori, or their gold-work along the Atlantic from the coast of Cuba southward.* The market place was still, though strewn about were cloths of cotton, grown in color.** Standing about the deserted market were long lines of laden llamas either quiet or fretfully waiting. All spoke of an unexpected summons.

At last He spoke. The Master had a voice deeply resonant like a golden stream outflowing.

"As I watched you, oh my people, I thought again of how I landed upon your shores and came to the temple. The priesthood, crafty and deceitful, would have slain me for their idols, but they could not and their knives fell from their fingers. I ordered the temple to be cleared of idols, and behold! the restless ocean arose, and with foaming fingers, cleansed the temple and left it shining.

"I found you sinful in cunning warfare; I leave you peaceful and contented. I found you dealing in human slavery; I leave you free. My well-trained priesthood will carry on all rites now for me. Baptismal, marriage and the last interment - all will go on. Why am I going? Why have I spoken so long to the traders? Why have I talked to the foreign merchants, speaking to each one in his own language? Because there are wild tribes in the jungles. They know not of the One Great Spirit who rules all men. They follow Him not. They still wage warfare.

"Ah my people, indeed I love you. Yet if you had a herd of llamas upon a hillside, and one little lamb fell into the canyon and into some brambles, would you not go down to save it, to comfort it and still its crying?

"So I go to save my llamas, for that is My Father's Business."✝

(*All found today - 1955 Ancient Peruvian pot in the ruins of Monte-Alban, Oaxaca.)

(**Found today on ancient mummies in deep dry tombs, but the plants have vanished, victims of war and fire and pillage.)

Legend given in letter by J.C. Tello. (✝Note last word is "work" as Tello translated it.)

He Who Is Called Waikano

THE DIFFUSING light of golden yellow turns to green. The emerald green is that irridescent bird, the Quetzal, sailing past in lazy circles, his regal tail floating behind him like the trailing robes of a monarch; the yellow green is of slimy water; the verdant green of leaf-hung heavens filters down a jade pale sunlight to the reptillian green of sinuous coils. This is the dank, warm jungle, swarming with birds and brilliant insects in a riot of verdant colors.

Up against the twisting tree trunks stands the Council-House of the Chieftain, the Long-house, the log-built Maloka brought to the north woods by invading Iroquois and copied often by the Pilgrims. This was shingled with heavy palm leaves.

Seated just within the doorway, each upon his striped blanket, was a conclave of the Nations. Before them stood the Holy Master: He Who Is Called Waikano. Softly the pale jade sunlight fell upon the white folds of His toga, slightly tinting His golden sandals, His soft curled beard, His light brown tresses.

"For twelve moons have I walked among you, while the sun swung around his circle. For ten moons now you have not battled nor taken human sacrifices. I brought you seeds and you have used them; seeds for drugs and food and clothing, spices and the warm sweet chocolate, as well as gourds for good containers. I taught you many ceremonies, baptismal rites and sacred marriage. I leave behind those who can lead you, for I must go on to other nations."

Then the leader arose and spoke:

"Dark is the sun, Great Waikano! Dark our lives on the

day you leave us, and our hearts shadowed with sorrow!"

"Nay grieve not, my faithful people. In My Father's Land you will all have lodges, and beyond the veil I await your coming. Return not to your ways of evil; I ask but this: your faithful promise."

"Hear this, O Blessed Master. So that our sons will never forget thee, and forever keep thy teachings, we shall renounce the names we have carried, and to the eternity beyond tomorrow shall be known as the Waikanoes: Faithful followers of the Master."

The Waikanoes are a non-Christian wild tribe from Matto Grosso. - Author.

Orinoco Indians.

The Healer And The Tiger

AMONG THE TALL smoking volcanoes, among the mountains went the Healer, seeking out the ever-warring wild tribes, takers of men, the Sacrificers. He brought them seeds and lectured to them, speaking of the One Great Spirit.

Once on entering such a village, a little child came running to Him crying. Its clothes were torn and its body bleeding, clawed by the sharp claws of the jaguar. He picked the child up, and turning to the stream bed, knelt and washed away the blood stains. The people following in consternation saw no more the marks of the tiger. The child was well and clean and smiling. But when He held the baby to them, the people backed away in terror.

"It is accursed! Balaam is angry!"

"Nay it is blessed, for I have blessed it."

Then as the people still backed from him:

"Think you the anger of this creature is greater than My Father's goodness? Your Balaam is not so powerful; he must be fed the blood of children! My Father needs no man to feed him, yet He gives plants to feed a mortal. Plant seeds I bring you that ye may flourish . . ."

But the very man He was rebuking pointed with trembling finger backward, and the Healer turned - to face the jaguar.

Standing in the golden sunlight half dappled in jade from the overhead branches stood the tiger's silken body, its lemon eyes upon the Healer.

Gathering His robes about Him, and placing the child on the ground behind Him, the Pale One stepped toward the great cat and held His arm up in the Peace sign.

"Soft-footed Chief, in thy jungle setting, come close to receive My Father's blessing. Forgiven thou art for the

26

pangs of thy hunger. Go and claw no more little children.''

Then the people, standing awe-struck at the bravery of the Healer, saw a heavenly miracle happen, for the tiger lay down before Him, and rolled cat-like, to show its pleasure, inviting the caress of those slim, pale fingers.

The people, watching, fell down to worship.

To this day, among the wild tribes within the canyons and the mountains of the land called Guatemala, the story is oft-repeated.

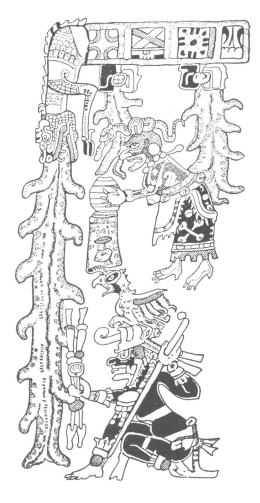

The Fire God.

The Priests Of Ek Balaam

THE PALE ONE went to Ek-Balaam whose location is no longer remembered. Here the priesthood of the Tiger waited to deceive and kill Him.

"We will offer to Him a captive. If He takes the sacrifice then He is silenced, for He goes against all His teachings. Yet if He does not, we will declare Him but man and kill him, and break His body over the Idol."

Along the highway to Ek-Baalam, capitol of the Sacrificers, came the Healer receiving the plaudits of the people. They strewed His pathway thick with flowers; they brought to Him their sick and injured; they cried His name; they touched His garments. Many were the mothers and fathers who held up high their little children that they might look upon the Pale One.

Past the ball-fields and the great parks, past the houses whitewashed neatly, past the well-kept gardens, past the markets and past all the business buildings went the sandals of the Healer and behind Him like a mighty torrent, running, pushing, jostling, shoving, came the multitude of the people.

He thrust aside the jeweled gateway with a gesture of derision. The first of the mob now seemed reluctant, for this was the courtyard of the Bloody Tiger. Yet the Prophet had neither stopped nor looked behind Him, and so, like a dam that is shattered, the people burst in and swirled around Him.

Quietly He walked on through them and ascended the dreaded stairway. Halfway up He was met by the blood-smeared black-robed high priest of the Tiger.

"No man dares climb these steps of the Blood God!

Ball court.

Come you as man, or a god from the Great Veil?"

"I come to you in the name of My Father - the one and only god of mankind. I bid you cease these sacrifices."

"Then you come as a god, and we welcome you as one. We bring unto you now a sacrifice to show you that we know you."

Statuesque the priests stood waiting, while the people in the courtyard held their breaths in mortal terror at the daring of the Pale One. This was the signal for the priesthood to drag a chained captive forward, bidding him kneel before the Healer. Before the priest could raise the knife to strike him, the Pale One touched him and his chains were shattered.

"Arise my friend, and join the people."

The people stared as if in shock, but not the High Priest. In a flash he raised his knife-blade and started toward the Prophet screaming:

"Thou art not god! You are a demon who fooled us. You cannot feed on life-blood! You are but a man with human pity! Die as men die - for the tiger!"

The Pale One raised His palms before Him and the High Priest saw in each one a large cross torn in the flesh. He stood as one transfixed.

"Why not strike down with the knife and kill me? Come now - ye cannot? Why do ye tremble?"

Then He turned and faced the people.

"Men of the Kee-chee, I bring to you a message from the God who has no image. He dwells beyond the rainbow. He lives in the lava, moves in the oceans, breathes in the wind storm and made all things from ant to tiger.

"There are but two trails to follow. One is the Way Of My Father and one is the Way Of The Jungle. You have chosen to follow the latter.

"Think you there is power in that image? That rock has only the power that you give it."

And whirling around He picked up the now fallen long knife, the knife of sacrificing, and smashed it upon the face of the idol.

"That is how strong is your Law Of The Jungle: the eat or be eaten, kill or be tortured - death ends all and so let us forget it and obey the law of our stomachs!

"You think of yourselves as strong men who crush and take from a weaker neighbor. Stop and look down the vistas of history. Where are the nations who lived by the Jungle? Where is the world-encircling power of the Serpents? It was crushed by the flood of My Father's making. Where are your strong men who lived by evil? They face judgment for breaking the Great Law of My Father, greater than all earthly precepts.

"That law is this: Love One Another."

The God Of Wind And Water

ONE OF THE greatest miracles attributed to the Prophet took place in Panuco along the shores of the Sunrise Ocean.

The Healer knew that the legends told to the children about fighting animals were in truth the histories of the People, passed down thus through the generations. Only upon attaining manhood and the status of the warrior, would the child learn the truth of these well-known stories.

Often He had read these ancient histories, and discussed them with the priesthood. Well He knew that the name "Serpent" stood for the earth's sea-people who had once with their fleets ruled the oceans, and established colonies on many shorelines. He knew that the word stood for water, even as did His first name Wako - Wah meaning water and Co for serpent. It was a tribute to His power over the ocean when at His command it had cleansed the temple at Pacha-camac.

One of His favorite books was that ancient history which had come down to His time through many ages from the day when the Red Land, which had fathered the Serpents, their colonies and fleets of ocean-going vessels, went down in the fury of volcanic destruction into the cold green depths of the ocean. "Proof that I am a Serpent" by the last remaining grandson to leave the doomed homeland, with its eye-witness description by the young prince from the House of Votan, was often read by the Prophet. Yet closing its pages, He would warn the puzzled priesthood to copy it very often, sending it to many nations, so that one copy might escape the flames, for when He touched it, He saw its final destruction in a holocaust which turned it to

31

Monjas, Chichen Itza.

ashes. (Note: It was burned by the conquering Spanish.)

Up to now Great Serpent had been His only title, because of his amazing power over water.

In long forgotten ages the islands of the Serpents had been beset by another totem. These were the men of the Wind God. They twined feathers in their hair and shot with bows and arrows against the poisoned lances of the Serpents. Finally this ability to kill at a distance overcame the proud sea-kingdom already harassed by the Fire God which it worshipped, and the victor was the Bird Of The Lightnings, known around the world as the Condor.*

Most deeply did the Serpents respect Him for His con-

*Lost in the silt of long dead ages was this time when the Condor fought the Serpent, yet the people of each land had never forgotten, and the ancient hatred was everywhere faced by the Prophet.

trol of the mighty ocean, but the men of the Bird of Thunder and Lightnings were skeptical of the power of the Prophet. All that was changed in one day of terror in the low-lying Land of Panuco.

It was a sultry day. The air was heavy, and all the animals were taking cover. There was a feeling in the air of tense

Modern Central American Indian.

expectation as if something enormous was about to happen. Along the sea the people were gathering, staring at each other with frightened faces.

"Last night the Giant Condor* was seen, the Thunder Bird who lives with the lightnings. He swooped very low and flew landward, warning us of the Wind God's anger."

"Perhaps" craftily smiled one priest of the Wind God, "the Great One called by us the Breath Master resents the presence of the Healer, known to have a power over water."

"Yes, perhaps that is true," murmured the people, shrinking away from the sight of the white robes as the Healer and His priests came toward the seashore.

Then out of the heavens came the Giant Condor, more than the height of two tall men from wing-tip to wing-tip, flying low to escape the whirling death-storm, and streaking rapidly up the river.

"Again he comes! Let us fly to the great caves, let us all run inward toward the safety of the jungles, away from the Breath Master's fury!"

"All you who believe in the power of My Father will remain with me," the Prophet said softly, "and nothing which comes from the air shall have power to harm you."

So the people remained, kneeling and praying as He had taught them. Also the skeptical priests of the Wind God

*The Quichua Indian name Condor from the South American Andes is the same in several northern tribes. Of note is the Arizona Hopi.

remained behind to watch this madman who dared to question the might of the Death Wind, terror-stricken from other encounters but unable to lead away the people.

Then at last, all saw it coming. Like a giant black tail hung from the storm clouds it swept toward them across the ocean, churning the waves into watery mountains as it crazily swung ever closer.

When at last the first thrust of the Great Wind struck them, the Healer stepped forward toward it raising both hands high above Him so that all could see those strange palm-markings which some said stood for the four-directions.

"In the name of My Father who rules the Heavens, ceased be thy fury, calm be thy waters, soft be thy breath as the breeze of springtime. Thou shalt but caress these people - in the name of My Father!"

Those watching stared in unbelief as the tail of the monster, the swirling Death Storm, withdrew into the heavens, and the sun broke through the scattering dark clouds.

Then all the people fell upon their faces, calling to Him: "Thou art Hurukan,* the Mighty! Thou art indeed the

Great Wind Master. Now we know that thou art the Wind God."

But the Healer shook His head and told them:

"Of myself I can do nothing. I pray you call me not the Wind God. The power lies in the Great Spirit who rules both the wind and water."

Yet still the people bowed before Him, and Hurukan,* meaning the Great Storm, became His name throughout the broad land and from this time on among all the nations, He was known as the Lord of Wind and Water.

*From this name we get our modern "hurricane".

34

The Land Of The Woman

AFTER HIS VISIT to the city of Ek Balaam the Healer went to the Land of the Woman. The Queen of this land was lovely, cruel and heartless with skin the color of old ivory and hair as blue as the wing of a raven. Her hands were as smooth as the skin of a baby, yet she ruled with a fist of iron, and there was none to gainsay her.

When her scouts informed her that the "Great Healer" was coming, her eyes narrowed and her smile was that of the tigress.

"If we do not greet this stranger," she told her courtiers as she called them into council, "the people may turn at last against us, for they think Him divine, and as you know, they have named Him, among other titles, the Lord of Wind and Water. On the other hands, if we do entertain Him, and allow Him to fashion a temple, He may change our manner of living, or so devoutly win the people that they will no longer obey us. Therefore we cannot entertain Him."

"Then off with His head," shouted the courtiers.

"Nay, not so fast; it is said that none can touch Him, for His eyes hold His enemies like one frozen in a trance."

"Then we will ambush Him with arrows."

"Have you not forgotten something? At His wish, the wind and air obey Him."

"We still have another weapon. With poisoned lances, we shall spear Him."

"You would use the Serpent's weapon? Remember, He can walk on water."

The Courtiers stood abashed before her.

"You mean there is no way to kill Him?"

"There is one way which you have not mentioned. We

shall invite Him to the Palace. As a Prince we shall entertain Him. Then the night when He first eats at our table, He
shall be given the Seat of Honor."

"Ah!" The courtiers sighed in understanding.

"When He arises to speak unto us," she purred with the
smile of the tigress, "the guard at the door knows my signal.
As usual it is to be the clap of my two hands. That will
signify the trap-door is to be released. He will find Himself in a dungeon, and from this one, as you will know, no
man in all of our history has ever come forth into the
land of the living."

Thus was it planned, and as the Prophet entered the city,
the adoring poeple rained flowers upon Him, the Army of the
Woman came forth to greet Him and escorted Him in
splendor to the Palace.

He was given a room with a sunken tiled bath through
which ran an unending stream of warmed and perfumed
water, and upon His sleeping couch were laid out for Him
fresh clean garments made by the loving hands of the people
in anticipation of His coming. There were always many to
choose from whenever He came to another nation.

That afternoon, on the Palace rooftop, as He came out to
address the people, suddenly the mountain, over the city,
began to belch dark smoke from its summit.

The people turned, their eyes wide with fear, whispering
to one another: "Why is the Fire God angry? Is it because
He comes among us?"

But the Pale One, also watching the mountain, raised
His arm in His sign of Peaceful Greeting. With soft words,
He blessed the mountain. He spoke to the people of its beauty,
with its hair of ice and its soft cloud-blankets. He told them

to fashion their lives in beauty, so that when they came to the Land of Shadows there would be no unhappy things to remember.

That night all went as planned at the banquet. The Healer was given the Seat of Honor. No one seemed to notice that He spoke very little, that He toyed with His food, but did not eat it, and when at last the eating was finished, with all the laughter and entertainment, the Prophet arose and stared at the courtiers. From face to face went the grey-green eyes, until the silence lengthened into unnaturalness.

Then suddenly the Woman arose. Staring imperiously upon Him, she clapped her ivory smooth hands and the Prophet fell into the dungeon.

Thus had spoken the Woman. Then she laughed with high-pitched peals of laughter which echoed throughout the Palace, down the corridors lit by the swinging torches and up to the high-beamed ceiling.

At first uneasy were the eyes of the courtiers, then one by one they began to join her. Robustly the guards of her army laughed, and finally all the courtiers, but above them all laughed the Woman.

Yea, thus had spoken the Woman - then spoke the mountain!

With a crash heard into the enemy kingdoms, the whole

Sculptured figure over doorway of a building called Akatzeeb at **Chichen Itza.**

Kukulkan, The Thunder God.

38

top of the mountain exploded! Gone was its head-dress of ice-white feathers! Gone were the soft cloud-blankets! And as the tiger shakes the monkey, so the mountain shook the city!

Within the Palace which had rung with laughter but a breath before the explosion the great walls swayed and crumbled! Sputtering fireflies, the torches flew into the rubble of cement and stucco! Down came the beams on the banquet table, crushing the wildly screaming courtiers, clinging insanely to one another, even as gophers are crushed when Condora, the Lightning, crashes down a forest-monarch under whose roots had been their runways.

Only two escaped: a guard and the Woman.

Where one torch still was crazily swinging, she ran down the corridors screaming. Following her came the long shrieks of horror of the dying. Above the fury of the mountain and the crash of falling rock and stucco was heard that hideous prelude of death.

Into the streets tumbled the people. There they saw two single figures. One was the Prophet, standing bare-headed and gazing quietly toward the mountain. The other was a guard from the Palace, injured and burned from those moments of terror, crawling abjectly toward the Healer, babbling out an incoherent story and pointing toward the ruins of the Palace.

Into the streets staggered the people, carrying their injured and crying children, gazing in unbelief at the mountain, a flaming torch against the heavens, lighting the city like a red sun or a monstrous fiery fountain, flinging upward stars of fury which danced grotesquely about the crimson moon, and returned to earth in a blazing curtain.

On the ruins of the Palace stood the Pale One, His robe untouched by the rain of cinders. Then He waved the people toward Him, and turning, walked away from the city. Clinging to each other, they followed, stumbling through the thickening fog of ashes.

All night they walked away from the mountain, resting but once to crowd around Him, while He healed their wounds and stroked the burned ones, making whole the flesh beneath His fingers. Then on again to the land of Panuco, near a mighty river, where they stopped and built another city. Here a great pyramid-temple was dedicated to the Prophet and the mountain.

To this day, in the Land of Panuco, one can still hear the legend of how the Healer came to the Land of the Woman, and was saved from death by the flaming mountain. The Place of Destruction is called the Land of the Red Moon, and the ruins are untouched by the spades of strangers.

If one is trusted by the people, they will tell a curious story. . .

When the moon is full, say the people, strange things happen at the Place of Destruction. Strangers who go there and stay through the night, when the moon lights up the desolation, swear they can look into the Palace. There, a torch is crazily swinging as if still heaving from an earthquake, and a woman is heard madly running followed by wild peals of laughter which re-echo throughout the ruined city, ending in stricken shrieks of horror.

No stranger will stay there more than one night, and they always hurriedly leave the country.

Is there anyone who will confirm the story? No. For not one of the people could be induced by gifts or money to lead a party to the Place of Destruction when the moon is full and the Woman is laughing. So perhaps even the location has been forgotten, down through these many ages.

(Note: Of the two versions of this legend, the one that the Woman was banished to the Land of the Red Moon where she became insane, seems more garbled, and less complete in its story. Therefore this version which explains the name Land of the Red Moon seems more logical, and was the one chosen to be included in this book.)

The Thanksgiving Ceremony

IN THE Land of Panuco which, shortened from the longer name of the Ancients, means: "The place where the Serpents landed when they fled from burning Pahn", the Healer met many merchants and saw olden cities, some still living and some in ruins. Nearly was fabulously old Xibalba, now rapidly crumbling into the ocean. Into these ports came the traders who brought the copper down from the Northland (Lake Superior) to the Southern Sea and the Sunrise Ocean. From them He learned their language, and soon won an invitation to ride into the Puan cities. From their name He knew these people to be a lost colony from Pahn, the sunken Red Land, and He was most anxious to meet them.

These ships of the traders were made from a great log slowly hollowed out by fire and patient chipping until they could hold many rowers. Even into the time of the white man have come these fleets of the traders, as Father Mercier, in his travels with the explorers, has so faithfully described them.

Thus the Healer rode northward to an extensive city in the land now known as Georgia. It once had a name which was was changed to E-See-Co-Wah, which means the Lord of Wind and Water.

Famous all over the Americas now was the Mighty Master, and the people came from many miles away to see Him, strewing His pathway with fragrant blossoms. Here He built a pyramid-temple, with painted logs as was the Puan custom, and dedicated it to Our Father, the Great Spirit.

When He saw that the people were in a hurry to finish it, He inquired the reason and learned that a great ceremony was coming called the Thanksgiving Ceremony.

Concerning this, the Prophet was puzzled. Surrounding himself with His usual disciples, twelve in number, thus with Himself making thirteen, the Dawn Star's number, He inquired about the ceremony which the people wished to remember.

"Is it the same," He asked, "as the one at Panuco? They, too, have a Thanksgiving Ceremony, only it takes place a moon later."

"Yes, it is the same. It celebrates the safe arrival of Votan from the burning Red Land. His fleet came first to Massachusetts and they celebrate a moon earlier."

"I would hear more of the story."

"It is said that when the young prince of the House of Votan, with his large fleet first touched the firm earth, all did kneel and kiss the sweet ground with the grass growing on it, and send up a prayer of thanksgiving. Since that time each place which the fleet touched in turn has its Thanksgiving Ceremony.* During the feast which follows, we eat of the plants which he brought with him: we eat the corn, beans, and red tomatoes, the squash and mashed potatoes. We have melons with rich ripe strawberries and other berries. We drink of the delicious chocolate. For meat we have the deer, buffalo or the bird called Turku (turkey) for all these came from the Old Red Land now long lost in the floods of the Great Destruction."

When the Prophet learned of this, He gave the rite His blessing and made it one of the Feasts of the Temple, thus making the people very happy, for they thought of Pahn as their ancient homeland.

(*See Bancroft and others.)

The Prophet
First Sees The Future

IT WAS DURING this rite of dedication of the Pyramid Temple in the place now called Etowa, Georgia, that the Prophet first mentioned the future.

Standing high above the people, and staring off to the horizon, after His dedication speech had been finished, once more He started speaking:

"Afar off through time my spirit is walking down the cycles of the future.

"I see the armies of the Serpents moving northward from their cities, being driven out by bloody warfare. These ancient worshippers of the Fire have returned to the ways of their fathers and once more are sacrificing to idols. They are coming up the river, the Serpents led by the Turtle.

"The Puan people will move northward and an uneasy peace shall for some time follow, but a civil war will break out among them. Now if you could only convert these people once more to the Peace religion of the One God, and also those who are coming down from the northward along the Sunset Ocean, then what follows might be different. But I fear that you cannot. Civil war becomes anarchy and each city takes to the forest, joining in tribes for senseless warfare. Remember this and tell your children. Woe follows this unhappy decision.

"Farther off there is another invasion. In ships many bearded men are coming from across the Sunrise Ocean. Many are the ships as the snowflakes of winter. I see these men taking the Broad Land; and the Mounds which hold the crests of our cities are for them, alas!, but earth for the taking. They do not respect our trees of cedar. They are but hungry, unenlightened children, and with them the vision closes.

"Would that I could reach those war-hungry Serpents!

"Would that I could speak to those bearded farmers!

"I have tried. They do not hear me. They go on their way like spoiled children, while I return to you and the present here at the Temple at E-See-Co-Wah!"

Many Southern tribes now in Oklahoma, with the mingled

Seminole Indians.

heritage of both Puan and Serpent, still remember this prediction first spoken at the Temple in Georgia so long ago in times long vanished. Choctah, Cherokee, Chickasaw and Creek - do your children still remember? Or have the old chants been forgotten as they have among so many others?

44

The Golden Rule

Given by the Prophet to the Shawnee

"Do not kill or injure your neighbor, for it is not he that you injure; you injure yourself. Do good to him, thus adding to his days of happiness even as you then add to your own.

"Do not wrong or hate your neighbor; for it is not he that you wrong: you wrong yourself. Rather love him, for The Great Spirit loves him, even as He loves you."

(*The Traditional Chant.)

The Lost Faun

ONE OF THE most charming of all the Prophet legends, is that told by the Cherokee Nation.

Once, as the Healer walked in the forest, deeply troubled by thoughts of the future, He came upon a faun in a pool of moonlight. Its coat was blue and silver, its legs were weak, for it was hungry and it could not find its mother.

The Healer spoke to it: "Silver-flecked babe of the forest, where is thy mother? Which path did she take when she left thee?"

The forest child looked at Him sadly, then turned toward a dim path. Unhesitatingly the Great Man followed.

Not far away they came to a bower, and there among the leaves lay the mother. She had been clawed unmercifully by the tiger; but in leading away the huge cat, she had saved the forest infant.

The Healer knelt, gently stroked her torn and bleeding body until at last she stood erect beside Him. His disciples, who had been following Him at a distance so that no harm would come to Him, saw the miracle happen. They stopped and stared with eyes unbelieving as the doe nuzzled her faun.

"Art thou not afraid," His disciples said to Him, "that using thy power on the animal kingdom, someday it shall all be gone when most you desire it?"

"Nay," smiled the Pale One. "There cannot be too many good deeds. Such is the manner of compassion. A lost lamb is my Father's business, as important as saving a nation, if one need not choose between them. More precious in my Father's eyes is a good deed than the most

The Lost Faun.

exquisite jewel.''

His disciples knelt to touch His white robe, where the dark crosses stood out in the moonlight.

The Prophet Tells Of His Birth

THE SANDALS OF the Prophet carried Him to a city whose name has vanished in the dust of other ages. Today the name of Oklahoma, translated from the native language, means the Land of the Red Man. Here was a large Puant city, whose crests showed an interesting history, and to this metropolis came the Healer. Here He once more changed the temples, chose from the priesthood His twelve disciples, and lectured to all the people.

Here He was asked by His priesthood to speak to them of His childhood, and in some of the legends we have some interesting comments.

He told them that He was born across the ocean, in a land where all men were bearded. In this land He was born of a virgin on a night when a bright star came out of the heavens and stood over His city. Here, too, the heavens opened and down came winged beings singing chants of exquisite beauty.*

When the University of Oklahoma was digging in the Spiro Mound, much pottery was discovered which showed winged beings singing, and here was also the hand with the cross through the palm, about which the professors were deeply puzzled, and still have no explanation as they stare at these things in their museums. About the campfires of the Ancients the tales of the Prophet are secret. For the benefit of their youth they chant the stories of long ages ago when they lived in cities, and of a sainted Healer who came and lived among them.

To them, He was known as Chee-Zoos, the Dawn God,**

48

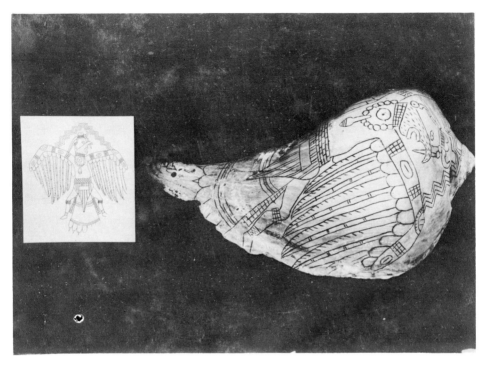

A piece of pottery found in the Spiro Mound, showing a winged being singing.

and they whisper of Him about the campfires on winter evenings when no white man can listen. The love they bear Him is beyond measurement, for well they know He watches over them, and that when their journey here is over, He will meet them in the Land of Shadows, for such was His sacred promise. They smoke the Sacred Peace Pipe in His memory, and blow the smoke to the four directions, knowing that to each man comes his retribution, no matter how flows the river of history.

Thus in great pride walks the Red Man, even though now dire poverty stalks him and starvation or hunger sits at his table. In the masklike calm of his expression there smiles a secret satisfaction, a something which to puzzled white men is entirely beyond understanding.

(Note: See the various scientific reports on the Oklahoma Spiro Mound.)

Background Knowledge

PERHAPS EGYPT knew of them as the Phillistines invading from the mighty Atlantic, once called People of the Ocean. Perhaps they were welcomed by the Norsemen who had known them as traders, and who adopted some of their legends; perhaps some of their words still linger among the Basques and Finns of the northland, both now an ancient islanded language.

Yet the mighty invasion of the Serpents fleeing from the Great Destruction washed the shores of the American tropics, breaking into small lost families, each known under its leader as a "Great Sun" whose throne went always down through the women. All counted their time by the cycles of Venus, star of both the dawn and evening. At the end of the one-hundred-and-four year cycle, and sometimes at the fifty-two year half-cycle,* their Great Suns met in giant conclave to check their time and pool their knowledge. From the snows of the north to the snows of the southland they came to pool geographical knowledge. And because He who was known as the Healer seemed greatly to revere the Dawn Star, the Serpents regarded Him as Holy, and they were ordered not to harm Him.

Perhaps in the days of the Prophet, Serpent tribe had not yet fought against Serpent, as they did through the later ages.

For the region of the Mississippi during the golden days of the Healer, Decoodah paints us a fairly clear picture. Those we now call the Great Mound Builders, were tribes speaking the word-family and branches of the Algonkin

(*For further information see Notes.)

language. These were the Ancients of the country.

In the days of the Great Mound Builders, these mounds marked the sites of the cities. The mounds were a sort of writing, a manner of recording passing history, a royal marriage, a dynasty ended. They were to be read from the inside outward, and about them swirled the cities. One had an even longer history than the modern town of London.

The mounds were probably faced with lumber and then painted in brilliant color, perhaps to resemble those of the Mayans with whom they seemed to have some commerce. In fact that commerce may have been extensive since there was much mining in Michigan.

To this happy and peaceful land came the Great White Robed Master with His sea-grey eyes and His golden sandals. Here too, we find the only relics probably touched by his hands or possibly fashioned under his personal direction.

In the Spiro Mound in Oklahoma, opened carefully in the practiced manner of all university excavations, was found the symbol of the hand with the great T-Cross through its center. There has also been recovered much pottery with winged beings not unlike the angels singing.

In the Indian mound of Pittsfield was found three pages of parchment now held in old Harvard, upon which were quotations from the Old Testament, written in Archaic Hebrew.

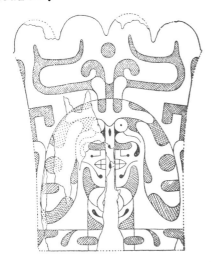

Bone object from a skeleton in Hopewell mound, showing a figure with copper headdress.

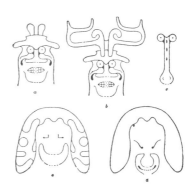

Same object, the design being taken apart to show symbolism.

About eight miles southeast of Newark, the father of Bancroft, Indian recorder of untold legends, speaks of finding the only engraved stone pictograph of the white-robed teacher. About His head, in Ancient Hebrew were the words of the Ten Commandments. His hair and beard are well pictured as well as His flowing toga.

It was a small stone, highly polished, an inch and a half thick, eight inches long, four inches on one end to three on the other. This had been placed in a casket completely watertight, and many feet above it was the burial of the Indian high priest.

How many other mounds have been plowed and leveled, and their contents scattered which the Red Men held as holy, planting trees of the sacred cedar upon them to keep them safe through two millenia? True, the invasion of the Serpents from perhaps 700 A.D. onward, coming up the Mississippi in their long snake-painted dugouts, carrying their sacred fire, brought an end to peaceful living, brought with them war and pillage and the priesthood of the Sacrificers. Yet they turned away from the hills of cedar, seeing the symbols of the Healer.

Serpent head in copper, Hopewell mounds.

Random Memories

THESE ARE a series of memories; a word or two dropped in passing.

The Pawnee remember the Prophet who came and taught them of His Father: the Mighty Holy of the Heavens. He told them not to forsake His precepts, and when they returned again to warfare, they thought often of His predictions, of how war but breeds more carnage. Even then He foretold the coming of white man. The Pawnee remember Him as Paruxti and His Father as Tirawa. They know that they disobeyed Him and they pray to Him in anguish.

The Algonkin of the Eastern Seaboard, when asked how they got their name for the Dawn Light, say that it was the name of the Pale One. They would not give Him their own name, as He had asked them, for to Him names meant nothing and He allowed each tribe to name Him. They asked instead His name in childhood when He lived across the ocean. The name He gave them was a strange one, hard to say in their liquid language, so today they try hard to say it: Chee-Zoos, God of the Dawn Light.

The Algonkin of the Great Lakes remember well the pale Great Master. The Chippewa say He gave them many medicine lodges whose signs and symbols are secret, fashioned from those across the ocean, and even today they hold this secret knowledge.

Even the proud Dakotah, they of the Turtle Totem, leading north the line of Serpents in their age-old migration, recall in long-lost adoration the sacred name of the pale-faced Healer.

"It was long ago that we knew Him. He gave to us our rite of baptism, many of our lodges, and our rites of purification. When He came to us the days were warmer; the sun cast down shorter shadows. Well do we remember how He foretold the coming of white man, and other predictions. We have backslid from His teachings, but to Him we dance the Sun Dance. We remember Great Wakona well."

Painted capstone from the Temple of the Owl, Chichen Itza.

The Prophet Makes A Second Visit To The Pawnee

MANY TRIBES have tales of the Healer, and how at one time He came among them. Few did He miss, no matter how distant or poor, or lost in the ways of other religions. But to the Pawnee He came twice - the last time in anger.

The Prophet had gone westward to that place we call Oklahoma, where the Puants had a thriving city, and there He was busy erecting temples and instructing a priesthood. Some wild young braves among the Puanee, who today are known as the Pawnee, formed a secret league to prey on the country, to make themselves rich by attacking the merchants and returning to the old war-religion. The merchants thus captured they would give to the Fire God, who would protect them, said the young men.

Accordingly, one night the Pawnee waited in a glen of the Mississippi where the fleet came to camp and rest on its long journey from the Southern Sea to the Capitol City. Quietly flowing was the Father of Waters when to the glen came the long-ships of the merchants, to discharge the weary rowers for a good night's sleep in the forest shadows. They suspected no mischief and no watch was placed over the camp site since the Puans had long been at peace.

They laughed and joked as they built a camp fire, and in noisy fun cooked their dinner. Then came the time of conversation; of remembering the long trip; small talk of girls in distant cities; of the customs of other nations and of the man in the flowing white mantle, of whom there was great awe for the miracles He had accomplished. One youth was a skeptic.

"It is strange that we always seem to miss Him,"

this young man sighed, "for I would like to see Him - this creature that we call the Dawn God, and others the Lord of Wind and Water."

Then the talk became hushed and the head man prepared the tobacco, starting the Smoke himself by breathing it to the four directions, taking a few deep puffs of satisfaction before passing it onward to the man to his right in the circle.

At last, each got out his blankets, wove a bed of branches for comfort, and rolling tightly in the blankets was soon asleep beside the low fire.

Then with the yells of Skiri, the Grey Wolf, the wild Pawnee leaped upon them, snatching from sound sleep their surprised prisoners, now forced to carry their own trade goods back to the camp of the bandits.

That was a mad night for the Pawnee, leaping and yelling in the firelight as they staked out two men for the fire-death, for sacrifices to the Fire God. Savage was the un-tamed dancing as they lit the flames about the Puans.

Only one old man protested. He pointed to the East where the Star of the Morning was rising, but the young men paid no attention. Who cared about the Star of the Morning? No one but the One they had called the Healer when first He had come to see them. But now that One was far away, His magic weak here, as they chanted the wolf-song.

Laughingly they pointed at the prisoners where one was dead and another dying.

"Let Him come and revive these men! That would be much better magic than stopping a wind storm or walking on water!"

Then a fire lit up the east sky, where cloud banks had been piled up, and everyone turned in wonder as consternation hushed the chanting. Suddenly He was there among them!

Like a creature from another planet, shining with a strange radiance, each hair of His head luminescent, a weird glow rippling from His garments and His sea-eyes flashing with lightning, He stood staring at the Pawnee People.

"Is this the way you keep my commandments? Is this the manner of your insult to the Spirit called Tir-aw-wa? I come to shield you from His anger, or lo, great wind would ignite the forest! And to ashes would be consigned the Pawnee Nation!"

While the Pawnee stared at Him as if frozen, a weak voice cried from the fire:

"Chee-Zoos, Master! From these flames, release me!"

The Healer turned and looked at the tortured man.

"You are free, my son. Walk away from the fire."

The burned one moved and the chains fell from him. Then he staggered toward the Healer, falling and clutching the hem of the white robe embroidered with its line of crosses.

Those who watched saw a miracle happen, one which they had said could not happen, for the man straightened up without a blemish.

Nor was all over, for toward the dead man moved the Prophet.

"Arise! Another day is dawning. Thou art not yet for

the Land of Shadows! Arise and return to the Land of the Living."

The fire died away and the blackened corpse stirred and lifted its head and its burned arms.

"Arise, my son. No chains are on thee. Come toward me and be made whole in body, for such this day is the will of my Father!"

The man arose and left the dark flames, staring at his good flesh with eyes unbelieving, murmuring over and over:

"To think that I had questioned thy power - forgive, my Master, an unbeliever."

Sealed were the lips of the Pawnee People, with both shame and the terror of a child lost and bewildered. Yet down through the ages has come the story, and sometimes the old ones repeat it on winter evenings beside the camp fire: the legend of the Son of Mighty Tirawa who came back in anger on a shaft of the dawn light, and by His presence, saved from extinction the entire Pawnee Nation.

(Note: Chee-Zoos was the Puan name for the Dawn God. The Pawnee have a different name. - Author.)

The Healer Travels To The Puant Nation

ROM E-E-CO-WAH to the place where now is St. Louis, in the fleets of the merchants went the Healer, to the capitol city of the Puant Nation. Spread across the Mississippi at the entrance of the Missouri lay the shining Puant Capitol. Its boulevards radiated outward like the spokes of a giant wheel, from the Central Hub where were the Crest Mounds. These had been built from the center outward, and recorded the ages of Puant history. When a dynasty has been completed, and a Calendar Period ended, the artifacts of the period, the significant facts pictured on pottery, were placed within, and the Crest was closed with a Mound of Extinction. Henceforth this one was not to be reopened, and beyond it in the whorl of the Wind God, running counter-clockwise, was begun a new Crest for the new period.

On the old Crests stood the Capitol Buildings, built of great logs and beautifully painted, as was Puant custom. On the sides of the Crests were earth-hugging strawberry carpets, mosaiced and bordered with garlands of flowers. The same carpets flowed about the dwellings of the people, circular after the ways of the Wind God.

Many Crests had been closed at the time of the Prophet, and the Capitol City was large, for this was a great trading empire. There were four roads of commerce. Up and down the mighty rivers; to the east across the mountains to the fleets which moved along the shores of the Sunrise Ocean; west on the highway to Tula, capitol city of the Toltecs.

Many were the goods which were carried outward: hides from the herds of deer and buffalo, sometimes embroidered with colored quills of the porcupine; carved ivory from the northland; baskets fashioned from white birchbark, and decorated with quill-work; and of course the red-gold copper mined by the Puant Nation, as well as many other goods for trading.

The Puants were very careful of their planet heritage. Never was a cow with young taken, and the finest bulls were always protected. The same was true of the primeval forest. All fires were ceremonially extinguished and in the most efficient manner, while suitable trees were ceremonially scouted for long-boat construction.

Unforgotten today in Algonkin legends is the time of the Prophet's coming, or how the fleets ceremoniously bore Him, and how He was always greeted with flowers. If the white man never hears these legends, then he doesn't really know the people, for a few still live in the time of their greatness, but alas, if they meet opposition or ridicule from the listener, the chant will stop, and the recorder's silence will end the story, perhaps even unto the Land of Shadows.

(See Decoodah and Bancroft.)

The Seneca Legend

"ONCE WHILE IN the Capitol City, the Prophet heard tales of the Sunrise Ocean and the Five Tribes of Warring Nations. At once He expressed a desire to see them, for much opposed to war was the Healer, so He went forth with the merchants. Across the mighty Alleghenies the Pale God came to the Seneca Nation. There He called the Chieftains into Council.

"Long He spoke to them on the ways of His Father, as He had throughout the Broad Land, handling the language with great ease. He explained His Peace Religion, then He asked of them quite simply: what was the reason for their warfare? The Fire Chieftains were embarrassed, for they had long forgotten the reason, if indeed they ever had a reason. Each warrior looked upon the other and none could think of a valid answer.

"Therefore He bound them ceremonially into a never-ending alliance. To each He gave a sacred duty to perform for the alliance, and then He asked them to smoke the Peace Pipe, filled with tobacco and cedar shavings, and to blow the smoke to the four directions making the sign of the Great Cross, which is a holy symbol.

"Never from that time onward have the Five Nations fought each other, nor has the trust He gave them been cracked and broken.

"At this Council was a Seneca Chieftain who was tall, for we are a tall nation. Like many of our people he had a lofty stature, and could easily look down on the heads of the others. Indeed the Prophet was not a short man, but neither was He as tall as the Chieftain. The Seneca, seeing that he was the tallest, and could look over the light hair of the

Pale God, rose and waited to speak.

There was a shocked silence. Would he presume to question the Prophet?

"The Chieftain looked upon the Healer.

" 'I have been watching you while you were speaking, oh One whom the people call the Dawn God. It is true that you hold a most strange fascination over the minds of men. I know that the people call you the Dawn God. If it is true, then you can prove it. Meet me here in four days in the early morning before the sun has shot his first long red arrow, and we shall stand before this door together. If the first red arrow of the dawn light, touches your hair before it paints my eagle feather, then indeed you are the Dawn God. This I give to you as a challenge. Now, for this day, I have spoken.'

"Everyone turned to look at the Prophet. He sat quite still as if in deep thought. At last He arose.

" 'Your stand is well taken. I will meet you here before the dawning. When from the Sunrise Ocean arises the golden light of the Dawn Star, I will be standing here before the Great Lodge. I will use up the moments of waiting to talk once more with the People - all who would care to hear me. For now, I too have spoken.'

"During the four days the Healer went among the tribes, and though He did not speak of His appointment, everyone

Engraved pipe found on **altar in Hopewell** mound.

Chief Big Tree

Quetzalcoatl

knew that He would keep it, for the Great One never broke a promise.

"Accordingly, at the time appointed, great crowds swarmed about the small mound where the Great Lodge stood open to the eastward. First to climb the mound was the Prophet. As over the horizon arose the first golden shafts of the Dawn Star, the Pale God spoke to the assembled nations. It is said that He always charmed His listeners, but now there was almost a breathless silence. Indeed it seemed the very trees were listening and also the assembled animals of the forest, so softly He spoke and so well did they hear Him, because of the silence that had settled.

Now the tall chieftain left the others and slowly climbed the small mound, taking his place beside the Prophet. The two eagle feathers in the hair of the chieftain projected well above the head of the Healer, but no sign except a friendly greeting was given by the Pale Hea-wah-sah, who turned and began the Chant of the Dawning. This was a Prayer Chant He had taught the people, which has long since been forgotten. Everyone started to join in and then, suddenly, a miracle happened.

"Before anyone else saw the sunlight, a golden shaft of radiant beauty came down from some clouds banked high with fire-light, and touched the curling hair of the Prophet, diffusing itself like a halo until He stood, a luminous creature,

64

painting all the ground around Him with gold.

"The people then fell down saying: 'Behold He is indeed the Dawn God who has come to walk among us!' and 'He draws his power from the Star of the Dawning.'

"The tall chieftain, seeing the Great One clothed in gold light, knelt in the dust beside Him and taking the hem of the Prophet's mantle, laid his cheek on the line of creases.

"I know that you think this sounds something like the Legend of Hiawatha written down by Longfellow, the poet. You are right; there is a resemblance. Once he was our guest and heard us chanting. He liked our stories so well that he kept urging us onward through his interpreter of the language. We told him many stories. When he returned and began to write them, he mixed them all together; but he was not trying to make fun of our legends - he was confused. We still honor him for enjoying the chants, and even trying to get the rhythm of their language. We honor him although Hea-wah-sah never sought a Dacotah maiden. That was a much later hero, who married with a distant nation.

"The meaning of Hea-wah-sah? It is He From Afar Off. It is our name for the Prophet, who drew His great strength from the Dawn Star. All nations know He was of the Dawn Star, and that is why, even now, no nation of the ancient people known as 'red-skins' will ever make war or fight a battle while the Sacred Star of Peace is still shining in the great heavens. They dare not, for it is the Star of the Prophet."

(Note: I no longer know where to reach Big Tree, the Seneca, or even if he is alive. He once told this legend to a child to illustrate the fact that the tallest men are not always the greatest. I hope that he will not mind its inclusion here.

Since there is a variation of this legend in Bancroft, recorded over a hundred years ago, it seems to be quite authentic to Seneca tradition. - Author.)

The O'Chippewa Council

BESIDE THE SHORES of Mishee-gahme is the forest still called Sacred, in the state called Michigan. Before his wigwam stood Dark Thunder, kindly Chief of the O'Chippewa. He was gazing steadfastly westward toward the water-reflected sunset, and blowing smoke to the four directions.

Toward him came the college student, the one the tribe adopted by 'blood-rites' and for whom there was warm affection. That affection was more than mutual. That child of the white race found all of these people charming. He admired the agile and cat-like grace of the dancers; the smooth silken skin of the women; the quiet beauty of their language, at times most hauntingly poetic in its phrasing. They lived in a world unknown to white men, a world in which the past was present; a past more distant than our histories. Upon their reservations, poverty-stricken and spirit-broken, the student was learning to see them through their own eyes – as the Ancient Ones and keepers of the Olden Knowledge. Their's was a very rigid culture with patterns that ran back to antique cities old before the rise of Egypt. There were proper ways to address one's elders, to enter a lodge, even to ask questions.

"My father, why are you blowing the smoke rings?"

Dark Thunder finished his meditation before he took his seat and began his answer.

"Because if you look across the water which rolls from the Bay we call Kee-weenah, you will see it is touched with sun-fire."

"Yes, that comes from the clouds of scarlet which the

sun paints as he leaves us to light the lands beyond the horizon."

"You learn well in the schools of the White Man."

"You hint that there is another meaning?"

"Yes, come and sit down here beside me. Know then that the fire-path of the water is that travelled by the spirits who leave this realm for those beyond the sunset. Long ago there came to us a Prophet. He asked each tribe to name Him, for to Him names meant nothing. So we called Him Wis-ah-co, and we covered His paths with flowers so that He always walked on petals. Now He does the same for the spirits who leave us and I was giving Wah-tay-see my blessing."

"Yes, I heard of her death this morning; a lovely young girl, her cheeks bright with fever. . ."

Sculptured heads, Casa de las Tortugas (House of the Turtles).

Mayan ruins.

"The coughing-sickness of the White Man. Once such diseases were unknown among us, but something in our blood seems to invite them."

"Perhaps in the blood of White Man is a substance which resists them, having been built up through the ages. Yet the blood of Red Man, having never coped with these diseases, does not have this resistance."

"Perhaps."

"But tell me of this Prophet."

"Who paints the water with long-dead blossoms?"

"The same. What was He like? Where did He come from?"

"Your desire for knowledge is a thirst never-ending."

"Forgive me if I am too inquisitive, but I have never glimpsed this knowledge and my time here is short. A summer vacation is of such short duration to grasp even a fragment of it."

"I know, my child, so I will tell you, though seldom do we speak of the Past during the summer. Perhaps because in the days of my fathers when we lived freely in the forests, the summer was the time for hunting and the gathering of fruits, nuts and berries against the rigors of the winter. Very well, let us speak of the Prophet.

"He was bearded, and pale of feature - without doubt a White Man. His eyes were as grey-green as still green water, and just as changeable in their color. He came to us one day at dawning and the light touched His hair with the sheen of red-gold until it shone like newly-mined copper. Yet He was not as the men of your people. This one was a god, with high soul-stature. If He touched a man who was wounded, that one became healed

Figure of a forgotten king.

"His robe was long and white down to the hemline which almost hid His golden sandals. Everyone wished to make Him white robes, for then He would leave behind the old ones, and all that He touched was enchanted with His god-like power of healing."

"Did He bring other priests with him?"

"No, He came alone. He organized the churches, changed the temples, taught the priesthood. Some say He taught them a secret language with certain signs of greeting. I know not."

"Why do you call him 'the Prophet'?"

"Because He not only walked among us, He also walked the realms of the future."

"Are you sure that He was not one of the Black Robes who came to this land with Columbus?"

"I am sure. He came to us when we had cities more than a thousand winters before the days of the Black Robes and the Long Knives."

"When you had cities? Where are these cities?"

"Below the cover of the forest."

"What a strange legend."

"You do not believe what I am saying. You think I speak to you with a forked tongue."

"Oh, no. I do not believe that you would deceive me. I am enchanted with the antiquity. Where are these cities?"

"The ruins have been scattered by White Men."

"Then tell me the location of just one city."

"The city which we call the Sacred is not far from here. Its history is longer than that of England's London."

"But . . ."

"My child, you ask too many questions. If I had listened

Feathered serpent in stone.

to my elders with half the interest with which you listen, I might have had more to tell you. But I thought too much of swimming in the blue sea, and running races through the forest."

"My father, for what you did hear, I thank you. Yet I must ask of you a very great favor. Find for me another chieftain who will speak to me of these cities."

"Why would you have us do this thing in summer, when it is not our custom?"

"Because I want to write down these stories."

"Just to spread them among the White Man so that he can laugh at us and speak lightly of things about which he knows nothing?"

"No. Someday, I must make a book of such stories, not for the amusement of White Man but for the teaching of your grandchildren's children beyond our time - many generations. Already there are few who can tell these stories. Are there any others around here that know them?"

"No. I would have to bring such a one from a great distance."

"You see? Soon all these legends will be lost. I would know of these cities. I would speak to the future - perhaps beyond our life-span; for a book is a bridge from the past to the future, upon which we stand for this brief moment."

"My child, you speak with the tongue of the Red Man, and knowledge beyond your number of winters shines from your words. Once we had books and priests to read them, but those were times long distant in the past. Books are of stuff which can be swept to oblivion. Since then we have placed our stories in the chants of our people, but now even these are being forgotten. Your oldest books to us are but of yesterday, and how long may last these papers of your people?

Yet, you are right. The chants are dying. I too would like to reach other tribes of our people and share with them our ancient history."

"Is there still alive a chanter of the legends?"

"There is one. He lives at some distance. Go now and let me think on this problem. Come back in eight days and we will talk further. I may then let you know the time of his coming, and if he will be willing to chant in summer. There may be more than one, and then there will be translators so that you may not miss the beauty of the language.

"Come back after the sun has gone eight times to the horizon and speak of this thing to no other person. Then perhaps during a night when a certain star is shining, we will journey back to the times of the Prophet, when the land was peaceful, and we lived in cities."

The student was new in the lore of the Red Man yet one fact became instantly obvious. Thirteen was the Prophet's number, although eight was also important and five; the number of their difference.

In due time came the night of the chanting. There were present many sages; proud old men of noble bearing and apparently all of different languages. Their names have long since been forgotten, but never the drama of their movements, and the melodic poetry of their phrases.

In a very poor translation, here are their stories.

(Note: I do not wish to forget the help of another, Decoodah, who told the traditions of his nation to a son of the white race in order to "bridge the times of the Destroyers" and died years ago. Together these men made the past of North America in the days of the Prophet come to life. - Author.)

MICHIGAN

An Old Chippewa Speaks

FROM HIS seat cross-legged upon his blanket arose the old warrior, Marksman. For a moment he awaited the tribute of silence. A mighty specimen of manhood was Marksman. Although in years he was almost eighty, his figure had the lynx grace of the young man. His long hair, neatly braided, still had the sheen of the blackbird, his teeth were as strong and white as his grandson's and his eyes were still keen for the signs of the game trail.

"It is well tonight that we speak of the Pale God, and fitting as well that we council with others, greeting our enemies as brothers, for such would have been the wish of the Prophet. I have heard some talk among the lodges that the Lord of Wind and Water was but a myth brought down by the old ones from times beyond our present reckoning. That is true, but what a strange legend! If the youth among our people doubt the wide-flung strength of this ancient story, look about at His symbols from tribe to tribe across the broad land.

"Have you ever wondered about the cedar? Why does every tribe revere it? Why do the high priests mix its shavings with the leaves of our tobacco? To enhance its power, they will tell you. And why do we blow its smoke across our bodies, when we are returning from the war trail? Is it not to ask His forgiveness, as was once taught by the Pale God? Why do we plant these trees upon the Great Mounds - those ancient histories of our cities? Was it not to warn all men that once He walked here; the Sacred One, the Miracle Worker?

"And the color of snow: among all the nations it stands for peace. Why is this so? Because He wore it. From nation

72

to nation He taught the people to live in peace and to speak in Council, thus settling all their problems. This was His way and the way of His Father.

"Why do we raise our hands up in greeting? Because that was His Peace Sign, a tradition which we still follow.

"Why do we use the Cross as a sacred symbol? Was it not because He wore it about the hem of His full white garment, and carried the sign on His two hands, those hands so gifted in healing?

"How many here have ever seen the Sun Dance? I know that our brothers, the Cheyenne and Dakotah, probably bear its scars on their bodies. Let us consider for a moment, this strange dance: a self-torturing agony of suffering as danced by the young men.

"The ancient ones have told us that once this was a flying dance about a high pole, and that it came from the Old Red Land now forlornly sunken for many ages below the green waves of the ocean. Perhaps it once belonged to the Wind God which the Serpents made a dance of sacrifice in the times long vanished, many cycles before the Prophet's coming.

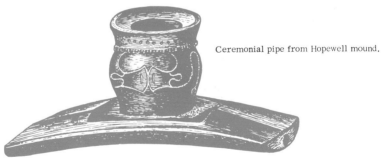

Ceremonial pipe from Hopewell mound.

"This seems very probable because the Prophet must have changed it and made it a dance of penance. Today as a sacrifice for their people, the young men allow the thongs from the tall pole to be tied under a two-finger-wide strip by opening the skin of each breast, then dancing night and day for four days until they drop and are again freed from the suffering of the Sun Dance. Is it not strange that we hang our young men thus in pain upon a dead tree? I know not why, but we feel that a blessing or a righting of wrong is certain to follow. Our tribe no longer dances the Sun

Ceremony of the Sun Dance.

Dance, but we still remember the Prophet. In the Wisacoo Lodge and many others there are some who still know His secret language, but those things are being fast forgotten.

"Yet to Him who walked away through the silver moon-frost, across the winter's snowy blanket, toward the North where now is Canada and many other tribes of our people, I bid you see Him as we saw this man. From the pines dripped ice like unlit candles, as He walked away. His snowy garments made Him seem wraith-like, while His long hair was silvered by His frost-breath. Two wolves followed behind Him; one of dark fur and one of silver. We knew that they would not harm Him for He had a strange power over the animals; the fiercest seeking the touch of His fingers.

"Thus He left us, and to Him I raise the Peace Pipe, the tobacco mixed with cedar shavings, and blow the smoke to the four directions, thus making the sign of His Cross.

"For tonight, I have spoken."

One of many Mayan pyramids illustrated on the scene by Catherwood.

The Voice Of The Dacotah

IN THE CHIPPEWA lodge a tall man was arising. With a lithe grace he shifted his body waiting for the murmurs to die into silence. In the full dress of the Dacotah, he was a proud and exotic figure as the firelight played over his costume. Finally quietness came, and the rippling whispers ebbed away to a sea of silence.

"Never before that I can remember have the Chippewa invited a Dacotah warrior to address them in council. No wonder seeing this costume there were many subdued whispers. Yet too long as enemies have lived our two tribes, and for that matter, all the Indian peoples. Anciently we came from the same homeland. Do you not read that in these symbols used again and again in our costumes? It is so through all of the tribes westward. Indeed it is time we dropped our dark frowns and learned to smile upon one another, seeking together our ancient history, for it is broken and shattered among us in legends, which need many retellings in many languages for the light of truth and understanding.

"I was invited here to speak of Waicomah, the Fair God who ruled the ocean and spoke in whispers to the wind storm. Our name is not the one you gave Him, for when He came, we lived far to the southward, where the sun makes shorter shadows and our cities were built on islands, many of which have since gone down into the ocean. After He left we forgot His teaching and we returned to the ways of the Fire God.

"As our land became scarcer, due to storm and great earth shaking, one tribe among us sought to be master. They began conquering city after city. We, the dispossessed who would not live in slavery to those who had our same heritage, sought the mountains, many tribes in council. From our traders, we knew of the Mississippi, and so in our long canoes, carrying our Sacred Fire, we began our migrations. We of the Turtle, keepers of the books and learning, led the many tribes of the Serpent up the great Father of Waters. To commemorate that we built the Great Mound of the Serpent led by the Tortoise.

Chief Standing Bear and Wastewin, in native costume.

"It is too bad that we had to take your cities. Many years had we lived in peace and traded, but sometimes we move but to fill the belly. Such was our move into the woodland among the herds which were to be had for the taking, and when one has hungry children those herds meant life. Such was our move up the Mississippi.

"Near White Man's town, St. Louis, where stood your great Capitol City, we built our Capitol. We did not destroy the crests of your building where you had written your history, we but added to them. White Man was the destroyer of both your histories and ours also. You realized our need and you moved northward; and there was peace between us.

"Then there grew up in the Capitol City of the Black Tortoise, Dacotah who sired our tribe. He had a great dream for the Red Man. He dreamed of a mighty kingdom, solidly one from the Sea of the Sunrise to the Sea of the Sunset. He could not gain the Emperor's attention and he left for the Northern Cities where lived your people. Now, though you had been a peaceful nation, his pleadings did not go unattended. Ears were opened to what he was saying: 'In the west there is much fighting. Fierce warriors come from the Northland, bringing great war-dogs with them. We call them the Men of the Coyote. They burn and plunder and carry away the women. Now I would force them into cities. I would conquer them and make them peaceful. I would build one mighty nation. As in the Old Red Land which we both remember, which was ruled by two together, so I would have you rule with me this mighty country.'

"In your cities of the Northland, you listened to the Voice of Dacotah. You gave him armies to train and your sons to learn the arts of warfare. Dacotah was a mighty general. He conquered the Tortoise Empire, and made his own mound after the Tortoise Mound of Extinction.

"He might have succeeded in his dream except that more of the hordes of the Northmen coming afresh down the West Coast decimated his armies, and then civil war broke out over the Dacotah Empire. Cities were abandoned and each tribe took to the forest, to raid and pillage and play at war games like naughty children.

"And remembering back, our wise men told us that once Great Waicomah predicted that it would be so, even to the final coming of White Man. Now when it is too late, we remember.

"You ask me to tell you of Great Waicomah. Our memory of Him is greatly garbled for so long ago was He living. We know that He prayed to the Dawn Star, and today, in His memory, our most sacred lodge carries that name. To the memory of Him, I make His symbol, and for this night - I have spoken."*

(*Confirmation of this migration legend is to be found in Traditions of Deecoodah.)

The Southerners Speak

NOW THERE AROSE from his blanket one who was dressed in White Man blue jeans. His hair was short cropped, and his feet knew not the Indian moccasins, but were clad in shoes of leather. He spoke slowly in the tongue called English.

"We are the Southerners. Formerly we lived on the lower Mississippi; we, the Cherokee, Choctah, Chickasaw and Creek. When White Man came we had log cabins built around our wooden temple raised on a high mound. We were the last to come up the Mississippi, except for the Natchez who no longer walk the green earth. Over the Trail of Tears* we were deported westward to the land of Oklahoma and there we met the men of the Osage. Our memories of the Prophet are dimmed by the ages. Among the Choctah, He was known as Ee-me-shee, the Wind God, for strange are the tales which are told of His power over the heavens, and the winds which speak with the breath of the spirits.

"It is said that He told us of White Man's coming, and when He did His eyes had a sad look as if seeing about Him the scenes of the future.

"Once He said: 'All my life have I struggled against this thing called the Law of the Jungle. Are these bearded ones who are still my children going down war's trail to final destruction, and thus give the last human victory in death to the Law of the Jungle?''

"He was sad that day as He spoke unto us, for He was leaving us to travel northward; perhaps to you, the Chippewa Nation, for this was before our migrations when we, too, lived far to the southward where the sun makes shorter shadows. . .

"We would find out much more about Him if like this we had many councils tribe to tribe. We would learn more about ourselves also. This I know: we, too, once had had secret languages, but I know not if they are still remembered. The women had a secret language among themselves. It was not taught to captive women. Then there was the language taught in certain lodges. That was the one He taught us. It would be interesting to study this language if this were possible, between tribe and tribe. It might tell us from whence He came to us, and how long ago He walked among us.

"In our land of Oklahoma where our plows turn the good earth, and our cattle graze on the brown hills, I have often seen His symbol among the women's work (who still weave baskets) as I ride to other camps trading. Sometimes it is woven with the Star of the Morning, or the Cross of Four Directions or the symbol for the Cedar, sacred Tree of Ceremony.

"Not only this, but something else comes to my mind. Once when riding my pony to another camp, I saw some old pottery shards sticking out of the earth on top of a large hill. There was a cedar on the hill. I walked up and smoked a cigarette rolled with cedar shavings. Then I picked up the shards. On them was drawn winged beings. Carefully I put them back and then I made inquiries to all the wise old men of different tribes. They told me that the Healer had said something about winged beings singing at his birth. Do you have this memory of the Prophet's teaching?

"This is about all that I remember. Except one thing. Even today, when we hear the weird music of the wind, we whisper to one another:

" 'Be quiet and chant the old prayers, the Peace Chants with which He opened the Councils, for that is the great Ee-Me-Shee chanting with the singing spirits in the Wind-song.'

"To his name, still unforgotten, still beloved among the people, I too, take the Peace Pipe and send the smoke to the Four Directions where His feet trod over the wide land.

"For this night, I, too, have spoken."

(*See Bibliography.)

80

The Legend Of The Sacred City

NEXT TO RISE before the assemblage was an aged man whose hair had been whitened by more than a hundred winters. Seldom does one see white hair among the Red Men, and when one does, it is almost a certainty that his snowy summit was attained at a hundred.

He was reverently introduced by an O'Chippewa who called him by the title of "My Grandfather", a term of the highest respect among the Red Men. His costume was unknown to my interpreter. The leather of whitest doeskin was embroidered by the dyed quills of the porcupine, and his moccasins were beautifully beaded. "Perhaps Sac and Fox, or Menominee," whispered my interpreter, "or again he may be of the Canadian Northwoods, or from a tribe now facing extinction of whom perhaps he is the last high-priest."

"How do you know that he is a high-priest?"

"See you not the wing-fan from the Sacred Eagle?"

"You asked me here to speak of the Healer, and the ancient days of our people's greatness. I was surprised to receive such an invitation. Are our young men having a change of spirit? Since when have they listened to the chanting? Have they ceased their love of White Man whiskey, truly known as Devil-Water, which looses their tongues and makes them foolish?

"Yea, it is true my heart is bitter, but I came not here to give a lecture. Let White Man keep his reason-stealer, for in time it will bewitch him. I came to take you back to the ancients and to the times of our people's greatness. I have thought of taking the legends with me even unto the Land of Shadows, but the young man who came so far to seek me, reasoned well before the fire. He said I had no right to take

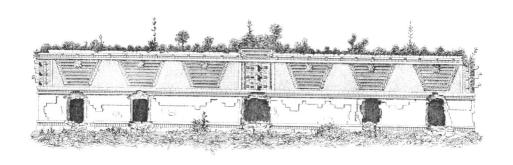

Uxmal - Eastern range of building, Monjas.

them, for they belonged to all our people as long as one Red Man walked the planet. They must go on past this generation and to that unborn soul who might be listening and wishing to walk back to the Ancients.

"Therefore tonight I am here to take you walking back through the Dawn Star cycles to a time long distant when the land was not as you see it; past the memories of our grandfathers' grandfathers. I take you with me to the days of the Healer, and the times of our people's greatness. These were the days when the Crests of our Histories whorled through many cities, always near the mighty rivers, avenues of ancient commerce.

"Coming north from our Capitol City, where the Mississippi meets the Missouri, in the long-boats of the traders, the Prophet made His journey toward the City we called Sacred. This was an ancient metropolis. Before we built its Mound of Extinction, after the Great Civil War of the Turtles, ninety-six dynasties of rulers had lived their long and eventful history. Like the Capitol, it too had strawberry carpets about all the buildings built upon the Great Crests, and from them the streets radiated outward among the dwellings of the people. This city was called Sacred because it was in the center of the Cross of Waters from whence ran the rivers to the Four Oceans. East to the Sunrise ran the waters, and Northward to the Sea of Dancing Lights; to the West beyond the Great Divide the waters ran to the Sea of the Sunset, while the Missouri and Mississippi ran to the Southern Sea, the Sea of the Karibs.

"To this, the City of the Great Cross of Waters, up the river called the Father of Waters, one golden morning, came the Healer. The dawn cascaded down upon Him as He left the ships of the merchants, painting His hair and beard with beauty and lighting up His lofty features.

"The streets were mosaiced with flowers strewn in homage on the path before Him as He walked toward the Temple. Greatly beloved now was the Pale God, known as the Lord of Wind and Water. His every move bespoke His kindness; His very touch revealed His divinity; and before Him all the people bowed down.

"Through rows of worshippers He moved to the Temple, in quiet solemnity, holding up His hand in blessing - that hand with the strange palm-marking, for through it was engraved the True Cross which He had taken as His Symbol.

"There at the Temple He abode among us, though He often rode away with the merchants, or more often walked to distant villages, holding in His hand His great staff, and stopping to speak with all the people, from the aged to the children.

"Once there was a great stir among the villages. Messages had been flashed with obsidian mirrors and the smoke-puffs of more distant signals. They spoke of an array of nobles who were coming to the Sacred City from a land called Golden Tollan. At first the people were much frightened, for though long had we traded with distant Tollan, yet if these emissaries were to be followed by their mighty metal-clad armies, the Puan Cities would be lost!

"The Prophet was the least disturbed. He gathered about Him a council of the merchants, and soon had mastered the Toltec language. These men in peace were coming northward, He told the frightened people, and shortly the messages confirmed his story.

"Before long well confirmed were his statements. Indeed they were coming to take back the Healer to the city of Golden Tula, a fantastic place of magnificent beauty.

"Grand preparations were made to receive the emissaries. Long were the lines of chanters; the dances most elaborate; and much practice went on with conch shell trumpets, flutes and tom-toms for the grand celebration.

"Then at last the day dawned and the long boats were sighted coming up the river. In the lead, as was proper, came the ships of the Puans, laden down with goods of commerce, and following them the ships of the Mayans and some other forgotten peoples. At last came the beautiful ships of Tollan. From that first ship came the guards all clothed in metal, and then a ship load of glittering musicians playing upon many strange instruments of music.* The last two ships were filled with the emissaries. Most lordly-stepping were these nobles, as they came down from ship's houses, and all the people were hushed with admiration.

"Long and thick were their emerald feathers, unlike any seen by the Puans, flowing backward like rippling water; their costumes were made of colored cotton embroidered with gold, with pearl and emeralds and even their sandals were shining with beauty. Proudly they walked behind their honor guard as they made their way to the Great Temple, where framed in the painted great-log doorway the Prophet stood quietly waiting with His shining hair and wearing His snow white mantle embroidered with crosses about the hemline.

"It is said that the strangers brought many presents, among which were snowy garments and a pair of golden sandals, which indeed He wore forever after. The Mayans, too, laid gifts before Him and received from Him the Blessing. However, when after four days passed the ships departed without the Healer, the joy of the people was tempered with sorrow when they learned that the Pale God had given His promise to go one day soon to Tollan, after He had visited first with other nations. The Mayans, too, and the other peoples, all returned happily down the river, for they all carried back a promised visit. For them this

(*Harps and a guitar-like instrument were pictured in Yucatan - Bancroft.)

84

was a thing for rejoicing, for it was a well-known fact that the Healer never broke a promise.

"The Prophet went both north and west with His long staff, in His golden sandals and His snowy garments, and nevermore was seen by the Puan Peoples, but word came back some four years later that He was on His way to Tollan where a kingly reception awaited His coming. He went by the way of the Chihuahua Valley which means the Highway of Ancient Power. Then came the fabulous tales of the merchants of His entrance into Tollan, when on a day that has never been equalled since among all the nations, the earth stood hushed and breathless when that wondrous divinity we call the Pale God walked down the highway into Golden Tollan.

"It is sad for me to retell this story, for the memory of the present comes through to haunt me as if in terrible mockery. Yet I chant it for you, the young men who listen and for generations will again retell it, on into the cycles of the future as long as a son of our blood still walks the planet.

"Thus for you of this night, and for those even more distant in time from those living this hour, I have spoken. In bitterness had I sworn that these pictures would fade with the brain which carried them forward, but it is true that I had no right to think that, and so I release them into the future, to that perhaps unborn soul who will listen and love them, as I when a boy would crouch listening about the firelight, and walk enraptured in spirit through a day so long vanished.

"I too have spoken."

The Cheyenne Speak

THEN IN THE lodge of the Chippewa arose a slender man of the Cheyenne. There was a brief murmur at his costume as the Chippewa recognized another hereditory enemy tribesman. Proudly he too waited for the courtesy of silence. When it finally came, he began speaking.

"Like my brother from the Dacotah, too seldom is seen the Cheyenne costume in the lodges of the Chippewas. We too look back through the vistas of history to the days of the Old Red Land when there was peace and commerce on the Mighty Father of Waters, known to men as the Mississippi.

"Like the Dacotah, we use twenty-six poles in our teepees, which in our language means mountains,* for we too think of ourselves as Men of the Mountains, who anciently brough their water from the snows of the high peaks in conduits down to our cities. The twenty-six poles are for each of the twins of the morning-evening star, giving each thirteen, which is its number.

"Like our brothers we remember the Fair God who foretold the coming of White Man. Yet so long ago .was He living that like the Dacotah, our memories are garbled.

"Four years ago I went to the West Coast to seek work in the motion pictures. There I met Indians from many nations, and all were courteous, and more or less friendly. One particular man, a Yakima from Washington, told me this about the Fair God.

"When He came to the Yakima people, they called Him Tacoma, and so greatly did they pay Him reverence that they renamed their highest mountain in honor of His coming.

"My friend said that when Tacoma left them, He

promised the sorrowing people that one day through the light of the dawning, He, Tacoma, would return to them. Through the long vistas of the moon, the sun and the dawn star, the people still remembered this promise and always faithfully watched for Tacoma, and dying told their children to keep on watching.

"Then one time a great ship came into the harbor. On the deck were men who were bearded, carrying rods which killed at a distance. The people were alarmed and amazed, but their chief, who was named Seattle, reminded them of the Fair God who had not told them the manner of His coming. So to the ship they brought presents, food of all kinds and cool fresh water, carved work and other trinkets. The bearded ones took the presents, smiled and were friendly, but they sailed away without remaining.

"Many years later the people learned that this was not Tacoma, but Sir Francis Drake of England.

"As my friends listened to this story, there was among them a man from Hawaii. He told a similar story. Once there came to them the Fair God whom they called Wakea.

The killers of Captain Cook.

This god-like one healed the injured, raised the dead, walked on water and taught the people. When Wakea left, said the Polynesian, He promised that some day He would come back to them through the dawn light.

"Through countless generation cycles the people still remembered, teaching their babes and then their grand-children to keep watching the dawns for Wakea's coming.

"One time a great ship came to them. The people met it with rejoicing, bringing presents to the bearded White Men, fruits and food and entertained them with feasting. Yet the White Men did not remain among them. They sailed away and the people, embittered, wondered if Wakea had rejected His people. True, they had not entirely lived up to His teachings. There had been some war and fighting, but on the whole through the long, long years, they had tried to remain faithful.

"That night a great storm struck the island. Was this another sign of Wakea's displeasure? The people were hurt as they thought upon it. Then they saw the ship returning. It was running like a frightened dog for cover, heading back to the safety of the harbor.

"Now the people knew that this was not Wakea. The Fair God had full command of the sea and windstorms. He had but to hold high that slim hand and the mightiest storms obeyed Him. These men were but imposters pretending with their beards to be Wakea! So the surprised White Men met an army of warriors who swarmed over the ship and killed the explorers.

"It was years later that the Polynesians learned the truth of this story of misunderstanding. These men probably had never heard of Fair Wakea. This was but James Cook, the explorer, trying to map the wide Pacific for a distant island named England.

"For this night, I have spoken."

(*Note: The name teepee or tipi, the Buffalo-hide lodges of the Plains Tribes, is similar in meaning to tepec, the Nahuatl or Aztec word for mountain.)

MICHIGAN

The Council Is Closed

THE LAST MAN ended his story and sat down, with the final expression: "Tonight, I have spoken."

Then our host arose - Dark Thunder. Slowly he looked about him in the tent where we sat around the great fire. Outside the wind sang through the leaves of the forest, and the sound made a sighing music.

"My heart is heavy to hear these stories. The feathers of my soul are drooping. Yet almost as if foretelling the present is the manner of the Prophet's going. He left our people one night when it was snowing. He was to go to the Cree northward to Canada, and after seeing the People northward, would turn toward the sunset and the Western River running toward the Sunset Ocean.

"They say that as He walked onward, the snowflakes danced through the skies in patterns. There were two wolves which were always with Him and now they followed His footsteps. One was white and one was dark silver.

"He had laughed when they had offered to guide Him, for He had often gone with the merchants and He knew the country well. Thus the People saw Him leaving in an aura of dancing snowflakes where was before a living forest - like ours tonight.

"He faded into the whiteness like a wisp of smoke is lost in the snowstorm, leaving only millions of moving snowflakes swirling about in fantastic patterns.

"Remembering this and how He predicted the distant coming of White Man 'Like the snowflakes which blow in from the Ocean', I am suddenly stricken with sorrow.

"Once we lived in the wild free forest on a planet just as the Great Spirit made it. Now that world is changed and sullied, and the Red Man walks away sadly through millions of engulfing snowflakes - lost like a wisp of smoke in the snowstorm.*

"For this night I have spoken."

Exterior of the Casa del Gobernador.

(*Taken from college notes made while attending this Council - August, 1918.)

The Western Seaboard

IN MICHIGAN, according to Decoodah, is the ancient center of the Giant Cross of Waters. To the south goes the Mississippi; to the north, the river to the Pole Star ocean; to the east, the waters to the sunrise; and farther west, those to the sunset.

Along this trail toward the sunset trod the Master's golden sandals. No tribe was too remote for His sacred visits, none too poor for His ministrations, none too war-like for His councils. If He heard of a war, He went there, called the chieftains into conclave, divided up the territory, gave them seeds and taught them gardening. "Do not kill unless you are hungry, and then ask the animal's forgiveness, and explain your great need to him before ever you pull the bow-string." This was a rule that never a Red Man would be so rash as to violate. So before the hunting each tribe holds a prayer-dance of olden ritual.

Always He was called the Feathered Serpent, Emeeshe-totl or Ee-see co-tl among the Algonkins (Tl means Lord). Always He wore the long white toga, embroidered with black crosses along the bottom, and walked through the dust with golden sandals. Whenever the people made Him new garments, He left with them the old ones, which they treasured beyond all wampum, saying that to touch them was healing. During each of His visits He trained twelve disciples, and one to be their leader, who would accede to His title after He had gone about "My Father's Business".

After His visit the grieving tribesmen carved the hand with the T cross upon the walls of canyons so that none would forget Him, and they could show to their children's children the eternal emblem of His coming.

To the Chinooks, the Prophet came. Once, when leaning on his long staff, He pointed to the plain below them.

"Down through the cycles of the Dawn Star I see below us spread a city which shall be named Tacoma. It is a city of the White Man."

"What are you saying, Master? Your name is Tla-acomah meaning Lord Miracle Worker. The Great White mountain where sleeps the Fire God bears your name, Tla-acomah - not the plain below us."

"Yea, but the mountain bears another name, and few of the men who live in the city and use the name Tacoma will understand the olden meaning."

The hot-springs of Tacobya mark the passage of the Healer, while in the canyons of nearby Coso, where so lightly sleeps the Fire God, there is a Canyon of Ancient Recording and in this long and silent gallery is the hand with the T cross and near it the Great Cross - olden symbol of the Master.

To the Land of the Havasu the Healer came one early dawn. Climbing down a steep trail into the Great Dividing Canyon, with the sunrise sun behind Him, they saw He of the White Robe coming.

The flame of the dawn touched His golden sandals, and long before they saw Him raise one arm in greeting, meaning Peace and Prosperity to You, they whispered to one another:

"He comes to us! The Great Tacobya! The mighty Master Miracle Worker!"

Then with the whole tribe watching, they saw Him stop and tap a large rock in the midst of the desert dryness with his long staff, and behold there gushed forth water. He stooped and drank from the Sacred Water which is still called the Spring of Tacobya.

To the Pueblos Tla-acoma came, who then were the outpost cities of the great Empire of Tula, capitol city of the Toltecs. Their lands were peaceful, their plantations extensive. In those days they did not need to hide on mesas to keep away from wicked raiders, for long was the lance of the Toltec armies to protect their outposts.

To the Wallapai Tribe came Great Ta-copah, who gathered the chiefs in giant conclave, and re-distributed the grain fields. Then He taught them more clever gardening, gave them melon, pumpkins and mescal, squashes and beans. He showed them how to conserve water in hidden underground reservoirs. Many other plants He gave them which have been lost throughout the ages.

To the People of the White Rock He came. They told Him that they had come here after the Great War in the Southland, where all their cities were left burning and they themselves but a splinter of a once mighty power. Sad in their hearts and ever homesick, they remembered their disaster. They say that He told them of another nation which had to flee oppression in days long-vanished. Then He showed them the beauty of their new land and how to make their gardens prosper.

When He was ready to leave the Pueblos, again He called the chiefs to Council. When He told them he was going, they were desolate with sadness.

"Heavy our hearts and dark our future on that day when you will leave us, for there are tribes westward known to men as the Sacrificers. Some day they will overwhelm us."

"Then unto these Serpent People will I go, and I will teach them."

"Yea, but will nevermore we see you?"

"In truth I give to you a promise. Keep you my precepts, forsake all warfare and you shall ever have my blessing even beyond White Man's coming, and woe to the hands that are raised against you."

"But will you come back to us, Great Master?"

"Yea, if to my teaching you are faithful, and to show that you have lived each day rightly, leave a light at night burning against the time I will return through the Dawn Light, and lead thee unto My Father's Kingdom."

So every night a light is burning in Acoma and other Pueblos among these tribes which we call heathen.

The Feathered Serpent Symbol at the San Idelfonso Pueblo, home of a tribe world famous for their black pottery.

93

ARIZONA

The Hopi Snake Priest

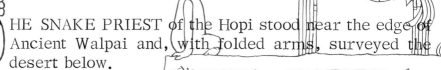

T HE SNAKE PRIEST of the Hopi stood near the edge of Ancient Walpai and, with folded arms, surveyed the desert below.

"Thank you for the Condor feather. You say you got it from the Great Zoo? For us it is a bird of legend."

"It is that for all the tribes of the American Indian people," I told him.

Behind him the old fortress upon the mesa top made a background for his figure, beautifully clothed in his native costume. His skin, light for that of many red-skinned people, was as innocent of hair as the cheek of a young child. That fact, with this beardless people, proved that he had no blood of White Man.

For a moment we continued to stand in silence. To speak too soon or abruptly would prove only that one had little breeding in the quiet ceremonious world of the Red Man. So I continued to stare at the ancient mud-brick city, already old when the Aztec monarch first heard of White Man's coming.

"You wrote to me in your letter that you wished to speak to me of the Pale God? Of those days now, few men remember."

"That I have learned. Yet I would put those days in a book for reading so that young Red Men will remember the Ancients, the heritage of all you people."

He sighed and glanced back at the Pueblo.

"Perhaps in your book you will write of my people; of their kindness, their old traditions, their peaceful ways and their love of beauty. We belong here on the desert."

"It is a wild land," I murmured.

"It is our land, and without it, life would not be worth living."

"Ah, yes. The desert has a strange fascination."

"It is easy out here to believe in the Fire God," he said, pushing back his long hair, raven-blue as the wing of a wild bird, and held from the eyes by a scarlet head-band. "Look at those mountainous shafts of red rock, torn and shattered and twisted upward. Here is a strange sort of soul-magic; a land of weird fascination."

"A never-never land of beauty?"

"I said it was easy to believe in the Fire God. See how he crushed and mauled the mountains? Then twisted them up.

"Even the water holes, cool and turquoise, are not always filled with good water. You can tell by looking for the animal skeletons."

"And the heat-waves paint strange pictures for the thirsty? Yes, I too know the desert."

"You should not have come to us in summer. It is not the time to speak of the Ancients, but there are some hints that I can give you. It is well that you move among the Nations. Ask the High Priest in winter. Perhaps he will not turn his back upon you, if he believes that you are honest and do not come to make fun of these stories. And when you yourself walk the Broad Land, remember that He was here before you. Learn to see His sign when it is carved in the canyons. Learn to know His name when you hear it spoken.

"Above all remember that He loved this beauty; for it must have gripped His heart with talon fingers when, alone in the immensity, He watched the sunrise or the sunset. Remember this when the sun-god is painting, and you go forth to speak to the people of Tah-co-pah, the Healer.

"Speak of this when you talk to the people and they will open their hearts to you when they see that your path of life is not crooked, but open and filled with beauty. They will speak and send you away with a blessing: 'May the Great Spririt walk with you down a life path of beauty even as I say it now in our ancient language: Lolomi, forever, Lolomi.

"Speak of this and you speak of the Prophet.

"Speak like this and you will hear of the Prophet."

The Untamed Seri

PERHAPS TO NO tribe is the memory of the Master more a living thing than it is with the Seri; the shaggy haired, neglected Seri, living in poverty-stricken squalor upon Mexico's Triburon Island. Still ruled by their sacrificing priesthood are the hardy untame Seri; still painting their cheeks with the ancient totem which came north on the balsa-migrations.

Thousands of years ago, say the Chanters, the Seri were part of the Serpent People, living together with the Turtles in their powerful ocean homeland, long before the time of the Deluge. After the great disaster, they fled to the land called the Snows of the Southland. Here they built giant cities and called themselves the Men of the Mountains. Underneath their powerful cities were the giant caverns of the Serpent.

After many ages a northern army came down and burned those cities and then the Serpents fled through the Caverns to where their ships were waiting, and took themselves on the seas to other coastlines in a series of long migrations.

To them came Tlazoma, the Miracle Worker, in a canoe which moved by wind power. He stepped out on the beach in the early dawn. They marvelled at His long white toga, His hair and beard gleaming with red lights, and His eyes the color of deep-sea water. They thought of Him as a beautiful teacher who suddenly took on the halo of godhood. That happened on the hour of arrival.

A man rushed out and fell before Him crying:

"Ahunt Azoma, Lord Miracle Worker - for you strange rumors have come to us - heal these eyes for so long darkened. Bring back my sight of the trees and flowers, of the sea and the people all about me!"

The Master, stooping quickly, gathered in His hands some

Hair Dance.

97

wet sand and placing it over the eyelids of the sightless man said softly:

"Go thee out and bathe in the ocean."

With breathless awe the Seri gathered. Here was the test. If he who had been blinded came back to them seeing, then indeed was a god among them. If not, then there would be a sacrifice for the Snake God.

The blinded man gave a scream of anguish, then a cry of unutterable joy, and came toward them running wildly. Looking at handsful of water, and at his curled fingers, at the sea and the sky, sobbing wildly he fell at the feet of the Healer. The Seri, watching, fell down and worshipped, calling: "Ahunt Azoma - Lord Miracle Worker."

For many moons the Master lived with them, teaching them how to store their water in their giant clay-baked ollas. He taught them how to feed their children after their mother had weaned them so that fewer would die as little toddlers. He pointed out to them many wild plants that could be prepared for cooking.

Up to the time of the Prophet's coming, and some say now, the tribe controlled its population so that it would not over-run the island or deplete the food supply by allowing no children life beyond that number which the death of elders provided.

This ancient law was broken by the Master as against the Law which He gave them: "Raise not the knife in bloody slaughter."

When the time came for the Prophet's going, He called the Seri to sit in council.

"I am leaving you prosperous and happy, but other tribes need me, so I go to the Papago."

"Nay Lord, go not to the Papago, they are an enemy tribe of wicked people."

But the Master answered smiling:

"In My Father's Land are many lodges."

"Then tell us Great Ahunt Azoma: You speak often of this Land of thy Father, yet you say not where it lies or in what direction."

Softly the Bearded One gave His answer:

"My Father's Land lies deep within you."

98

The Papago

EARLY ONE morning against the dawn light the sandals of the Healer came to the village of the Papago. The children had been loudly playing, and when the Lord of Wind and Water whom the Papago call E-see-cotl was seen approaching, the people were embarrassed and roundly rebuked the young ones.

"Nay," replied the Prophet to them in Papago. "Do not scold the little children, but instead let them come to me, for such is the will of My Father in Heaven."

Every day after that, say the Papago, He met and talked with the children. The Prophet did not live among them but made His home on a distant mountain called Bavo-kee-vulick which means the hour-glass mountain, for at this time that was the shape of the mountain.

One day E-see-cotl, the Healer, wandered into a secret temple where a child was being sacrificed.

The eyes of the Master went red with anger. He snatched up the baby, healed its gashes, and calling it by name, gave it back its breathing.

The priesthood stared and their arms were frozen. They could not move, much as they would have liked to kill Him. Stepping outside where the people were gathered He told them of the secret ceremony which was against all of His teachings. The people were ashamed, but afraid of the priesthood.

That night, two priests determined to murder this saintly man who was winning the people. They stole out in the moonlight for Bavo-kee-vulick, slipping knives under their blankets.

The moon was still up, yet the dawn light was coming as they neared the hour-glass mountain. In a part of His cave facing the Dawn Star, the Prophet was kneeling in prayer as the two blood-priests stole up the mountain. The

Matchina dance of mountain tribe of Mexico, showing both ancient and modern influence. Painting by Gilbert Atencio, age 14, Feb. 4, 1944. Member of San Ildefonso Pueblo, New Mexico.

Prophet arose and awaited their coming.

As they slipped into the cave with knives uplifted, the Lord of Wind and Water stepped forth from the cave into the moonlight, and faced them in their hiding place in the cave's dark midnight.

"Why do you not step forth from the cave and kill me? I have no knife nor rod to strike thee. Yet you cannot, even though in the moonlight I stand revealed? Know you not that you cannot kill me until the tasks which were assigned by My Father to me upon this earth are finished?"

Suddenly the earth began to tremble. The roar became deafening, and rocks fell downward, dropping like rain about the Prophet. Now the earth shook as if in a spasm, and with the roar of a hundred oceans the mountain collapsed,

leaving the Healer standing still on the rock in the moonlight. From within the mountain He heard two voices pleading for Him to go to the village and tell the people how the mountain had entombed them.

As the dawn light came, E-see-cotl walked into the village. All the people stood staring in frightened awe at Bavo-kee-vulik and then at the Prophet.

"Where are the priests who came to see you when the Fire God shook the mountain?"

"They came with knives before the trembling. They are still within the mountain, and from a great distance you can hear their voices. My Father has spoken in the earthquake. No more am I to live among you."

Walking away from them in the dawn light went white-robed E-see-cotl, nor ever after did they see Him.

Legend Of The Dene

ON THE WAY toward the people of the Zuni M'ahunt-Azoma met the Dene. These were not the tribes as we know them today, called Navaho and Apache, but a lost tribe of the wandering Serpents, coming northward along the mountains.

In the wild red lands of Monument Valley this tribe of the Serpents met the Prophet.

Skeptical of the Miracle Worker and the fantastic power men said He commanded as the Lord of Wind and Water, which they had heard from other nations, the Dene questioned His right to that title.

"Is the power of this One God, whom you call Father, greater than that of the Fire God?" they questioned. "His name no man breathes aloud, or the earth will begin shaking, and the hot rocks burst from the volcanoes. The Fire God ever devours his children even as he destroyed our homeland."

"My Father is a spirit who has no image. His power is greater than any other. Watch!" said the Prophet, pointing upward.

A giant rock which had been lying near them, half the size of a fallen cliff-face, began to rise slowly above them. The Dene watched, eyes wide with terror as it swayed and rose like a live thing, for had it fallen, it would have crushed them. Yet it straightened itself up slowly, and stood upended on another rock, gently rocking, slowly rocking, so that a child could have swayed it with a little finger back and forward.

That part of the Dene whom we call Navaho have another legend.

To the Prophet, names meant nothing, but they are important to the Dene. So they asked the Healer the name of His One God, and when the Prophet asked them to name Him, they refused saying that they knew not what name to give Him. Then they made a suggestion.

"Surely in your childhood, across the ocean, you were told His name? What name did they tell you?"

So the Navaho have the name He gave them: Great Yeh-ho-vah.

Today, White Man, hearing, is deeply puzzled.

The Prophet Raises a Giant Rock.

Pyramid of the Sun, Teotihuacan.

Pyramids at Monte Alban.

Temple at Monte Alban.

The Zuni And Yaqui

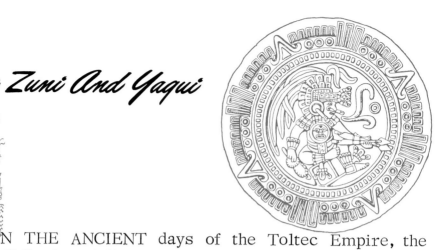

IN THE ANCIENT days of the Toltec Empire, the Chihuahua Valley was a garden, where today is barren desert. The Zuni and Acoma probably held the northern outposts while the Yaqui lived on the general trade routes leading to Tula through the Chihuahua Valley, whose Indian name means the Valley of the ancient-early glory. This might have been considered mere wild speculation in the time of our fathers, but today pilots flying over the desert can trace forgotten dams and aqueducts, and see beneath the brush and rubble mounds of unknown giant figures, like these of the Mound building Civilization which flourished along the Mississippi. So probably there was a connection between the copper mines of Michigan, now buried under a heavy forest cover, which dates them back to the early centuries of what we call the Christian Era, and the vast trading Empires which flourished to the southward.

According to Zuni and Acoma legends, they once held cities along the trade routes, and at that time spoke the same language. "The Acoma still speak the Zuni language," the old ones will tell you, "but throughout the ages, they have forgotten how to pronounce it."

When asked why the late Mexican Monarch, Mahnt-Azoma, received the title once given the Prophet, the Zuni answer: "When he was born he was pale of feature and in many ways resembled the Prophet. When the monarch was grown, and the guns of the Spaniards were flaming at the gates of Tenoch-titlan, he sent to the Zuni an urgent appeal for warriors to help stop the White Man's invasion. We sent many men. And though long we waited none ever again came back to Zuni. Now we know that all the Meshacan Armies

Colonade at Mitla.

were killed, and from Tenoch-titlan, in the Valley of Old Mesheco, our men went to the Land of Shadows.

"Why do I call the land Mesheco? That is its Aztec name and the Aztec name for its people. Their War God was Meshitli and they were really known as the Meshe-cans.

"The Prophet? He was a great god, a miracle-worker, a pure man of dreams and visions. We called him Great Azoma. He came to us on His way to Tula, Capitol of the Toltec Empire. In those days we were wealthy, living along the ancient trade route from the Puans down to Tula. That was long before the Serpent invasion from the Southland up the Mississippi or the Coyote invasion from the snowland of men carrying an Asian language. These great powers met and battled long until all the land became a wasteland. The Puans had to flee from their cities. Great Tula then had vanished, and the Pueblo people had to seek the high mesas to get away from the wild northern invaders.

"Of those times few men now remember. And over the Chihuahua Valley, where once was commerce, now only Tamesha, the Fire God dances in wild dust-storms, hurling the hot sand all around him."

Two views of Modern Mexico.

Mount Popo is visible in the background.

Mitla, Oaxaca.

Navaho woman.

109

The Chant Of The Yaqui

TALL SEDILLIO, the Yaqui Chieftain, a learned man in many languages, student of the Egyptian priesthood, far more learned than his degrees from college, who lost his life fighting as a war-chief in the last hopeless rebellion of his people, spoke freely of antiquity, knowing perhaps that his days were numbered.

"Yes, well we knew the Prophet. You see, we were the Atlantic Serpents, carrying on the Sacred Fire and our Sacrificing Priesthood, long before we were converted by this quiet, god-like person. He was a man very holy, filled with love, yet His heart was heavy; for in spite of all the honors of the people, the Lord had laid strange visions on Him. His eyes could see the future. It must be so. For as He predicted, all that He spoke of has happened. Today, though we go to the White Man churches, our true rites are to the Prophet.

"If I go to war, I know it is foolish, yet I have no choice if my people call me, for I am hereditary War Chief and carry the medallion of the Great Sun. I only hope that when I go to the Shadows, the Prophet will be understanding.

"Yes, I will tell you of those days and of Tula, the Capitol of the Toltec Empire. Wealth we had beyond the counting. Long have we lived in the Chihuahau Valley (whose meaning Chee is for power, and wah, very ancient), a land of mighty commerce and blooming gardens.

"We were the Men of the Mountains. It was our way of life to use irrigation and to terrace the hillsides. We brought the water down from the white peaks by means of dams and long covered conduits. We had sewers under our cities. We were a very ancient people. This was the manner of our living from a time beyond the White Man histories.

"Let us return through the cycles of the Dawn Star to the

golden days of the Prophet, Mahnt-Azoma, or Great Kate-Zahl. Most fertile was that travelled highway from the lands of the north to the Toltec Capitol. So lovely was its verdant beauty that it was called the Land of the Hanging Gardens. Orchards and ranches were heavy with verdure, and the great homes built of stucco were cool in summer and warm in winter. Flower and vegetable gardens covered every rounded hilltop where the streams of tinkling water flowed along in man-made channels and birds made the air sweet with music. Along the busy highway streamed the merchants, burdened down with things of beauty. From Tula came cloth of fine-textured cotton, embroidered with pearls and seed-silk, or gems set in threads of gold-work. Some carried paintings done with feathers, and some jewel work set in metals.

"Passing in the other direction, from the north came the copper, hides, and work fashioned in leather, or from nearer points, flowers or other produce bound for the markets of Tula.

"From the northland, where many tales had come before Him, at last came the sandals of the Prophet. Yes, long before Him had come the stories. From Seri, Puans, Papago and Dene, and many wild tribes living in the half-tamed woodland came these tales of wonder. Every merchant brought another, and they lost not one whit in the retelling. Tremendous fame had gone in advance of Him before at last He came in person down the road to Tula.

"Welcoming him with open temples, the Yaqui streamed to meet the Healer. The women competed to weave Him mantles, to embroider the crosses about the hemline, and the men to fashion new golden sandals, knowing that He would leave the old ones, strangely enchanted because of His wearing, a touch of which would heal the body.

"For Him they stopped all sacrificing. Instead they used but fruits and flowers to fill their temples, and then placed them on their tables, even as He directed. Indeed we still try to follow His teaching, although often it is not easy, and many are the times we have turned from Him to use the rougher ways of the Serpent, yet we know that we are doing wrong.

Monte Alban, Oaxaca.

"The baptismal? Yes. It was the Prophet who taught this. The godfather and godmother with their names of kinship; all must last for the life of the infant.

"For Him we changed our ancient dances. We learned new chants and ceremonies. Once our costumes were laden with jewels, and the finest of plumework was worn for its beauty, but today the people are very poor, often facing gaunt starvation. When we dance now with plumes of paper and bits of glass for the olden jewel work, we know He is understanding and forgiving. And sometimes it seems a spell comes over us, and the costumes of paper and glass change slowly in the light of His Star to the olden beauty. Once more the desert becomes Chihuahua and we see Him pause on His way to Tula."

Tula, The Golden

NOW ALL THE titles of the Prophet began to converge upon Him as He neared the Toltec Empire. He was indeed the Man of the Hour. Before Him lay the fabled city, known to men as Golden Tula, Capitol of Mighty Tollan.

Immensely wealthy were the Toltecs. Slaves and jewels without number came through the mosaiced gateways, resplendent in their pearl and emerald.

Vast were their chocolate plantations; endless their orchards of various fruit trees; stout grew their amarinth stalks, their nuts and beverages most delicious; and many other delicacies which today the Toltecs are lacking, being lost during the passage of the ages. As in the kingdoms of the Andes, cotton grew in all the colors of the rainbow and there was no need to dye it. So large were the Toltec corn-ears that it took a man to lift them, and the kind which has come to us, through the ages of war and pillage, is but the scrub-corn grown by the Toltecs to heat their baths of perfumed water.

Thousands of animals were bred by the Toltecs, from deer and buffalo to coons and rabbits. They had large flocks of geese and turkeys, ducks and other types of fowl. Many meats were in their markets and all men had a great abundance.

Of the features most remembered were the miles of fragrant parkways, filled with the sound of splashing fountains and the scents of exquisite flowers. Here the trees were filled with music because these enclosures were wire-netted, and thousands of birds whose liquid voices had been specially bred for untold generations lived there to enchant the listener.

Tuloom.

Here too were kept birds of rare plumage: here the bluish Xiuh-totl, glowing like a living turquoise; or again the Tlah-Quechol, a creature livid as the fire flame, or that which flew white and wraith-like, as lovely as a sudden-frozen snowflake. Crowning them all flew the Kate-Zahl, symbol of the breath of the heavens. Langorously posed the Kate-Zahl, whose tail, the length of a mighty warrior, was the jeweled badge of a hundred monarchs. Here it floated in easy freedom from tree to tree with irridescent luster.

Strangely skillful were the Toltecs in the fashioning of metals. Gold and silver, bronze and copper, and the finest of double plating was the art of their clever jewelers. Birds of silver that danced and twittered, and feather plumes of such a delicate beauty that many asked what birds had grown them, were on display in their jewelry markets.

Wealth unheard of was gathered in Tula. Palaces that were frescoed with pearls, edifices worked from coral, temples covered with the finest of gold work and edged with jade were among their wonders. Even their streets were paved with metal.

Such was the fabulous golden metropolis whose fame had spread through a thousand nations, and whose sight lingered on in memory in uncounted firelight legends for untold years after its fall and pillage.

Such was the world's most beautiful city, when the Prophet came to Tula.*

(*Partly from "Song of Quetzalcoatl", partly from Yaqui chant.)

114

MEXICO

Entrance Into Tula

WHEN THE PROPHET came to Tula, He was in the peak of His glory, because His fame had come like a ghost before Him before ever His sandals of gold had led Him along the highway to Tula.

"It is said that He paused on the passes, gazing long upon the golden rooftops, glowing in the early morning sunrise like a frozen sea of lava glistening in copper-gold eruption.

"Already everywhere the people were waiting, covering the land up to the mountains, lining the highways, singing and chanting. The stories had brought out the masses from a thousand miles far-distant, and emptied all the towns and villages.

"Long had they known that He loved flowers, and now they filled the air with perfume, raining blossoms down upon Him. This rain grew thicker as He moved toward Tula. Heavy flower-carpets paved the highway: roses, violets, tiger lilies, moon roses, golden poppies, showy hibiscus and dewy orchids lay, in the most intricate patterns, mosaiced before the tread of his sandals. Then as soon as He had walked over them, the people ran out and scrambled for them, hoping to keep a single petal which might have born His weight for a moment.

"From far beyond the outer ramparts stretched the homes of stucco, the edifices and markets of distant Tula. Some were built on the pyramid order, where one man's roof is another's garden. Usually they were filled with ferns and flowers, for the Toltecs loved their beauty; and tinkling streams of tumbling water, which ran down a hard tiled stream-bed from roof to roof. Now they were filled with Toltecs.

Tuloom - Front of the Castille.

"Then at last He came to the Great Wall. There in black and orange, gray and crimson, verdigris, blue and raspberry - every possible hue of the rainbow - moved the costumes of the Toltecs, flashing with their jeweled embroideries as they changed their places, or rose to see Him better. Along the wall holding over a hundred thousand people the Prophet moved toward the gateway where waited the courtiers and the Monarch, resplendent in their plumed head-dresses, to escort Him into Tula.

"At the gateway He paused a moment to gaze upon its fabulous beauty. Then He passed through the ponderous portals of metal, encrusted with their pearls and emerald, and from the throats of a million people came a roar like to an ocean, bursting through the mouths of the Toltecs as the Monarch bowed low before Him, and escorted Him into Tula, the Golden.

"He was led to the great Hill of Loud Outcrying, known of old as Tza-tzi-tepec, the last word meaning mountain, which then towered above the golden city. From here He was given a seat of honor where He could watch the ceremonial

116

Tuloom.

dances given in His honor, with the dancers chanting the Toltec welcome. But it was when He started to speak, that a miracle happened! Never before to a great distance could the voice of one man be carried, but from the hilltop to beyond the city, to the wall and on to the mountains went forth His beautiful voice, His musical voice, speaking in Toltec.

"It is said that after His greeting He plainly derided the masters, calling on them to renounce slavery. 'Do you expect,' the Healer said 'to enter into the gates of Heaven carried upon the backs of your servants?'

"Then He spoke of their enemy people in the light of understanding. He told them of his distant travels, and why there should not be war and pillage. He told them of these people they hated, and how with only love He had tamed them.

"No one who ever stood in His presence and heard that voice of compelling magic which swept away all opposition, could ever again forget the Healer.

"And so it was that day in Tula. The head-plumes of the Toltecs were bowed, and in mass were they converted."

(*Yaqui Chant, by Sedillio.)

The Bow String Of Power

AS THE Lord of Wind and Water, Quetzal Coatl, the quiet Healer found Himself the most powerful ruler on the entire face of the planet. For if Great Rome had clashed with Tula in that day when the star of each was brightest, mighty Rome would have met her master. No guess is this, but based on a Toltec secret: a certain means of hardening copper beyond the strength of White Man's steel; a secret which perished with the Toltecs and now lives only in tradition, that limbo of things long forgotten.

To the Master came the Bow String of Power. It was unmasked, and embarrassingly unexpected. His least wish was anticipated; His word was law; His desires unquestioned.

He set about choosing twelve disciples, as He had done with each previous nation. From among them He would leave a leader who would carry on His office, after the Prophet had departed.

He had a small pyramid uncovered where along the olden stairway were the sinuous bodies of giant serpents. These He knew were the symbols of water, so He ordered their scales refinished with emerald, shining irridescent among the goldwork in the sunlight. On their unlifted heads He placed plumes of gold and silver, of metal so fine spun they seemed not to be metal, but truly the wind clouds over the oceans. This temple He dedicated to the One God, whom He called the Great Spirit, the Mighty One Who Has No Image.

Then He changed the Toltec temples. Removed were the idols; gone the sacrifices; finished were the rooms with lovely mosaics, each room in the color of its own direction. South was finished in silver and living pearl, with scrolls of Paradise feathers, while the room of the West symbolizing

118

the Sunset Ocean was done in shades of turquoise and emerald with feather scrolls from the Xiuhtotl and other birds of bluish irridescence.

For Him they abandoned slavery, and they also changed their dances so that the anciently honored rituals became instead rich living prayers moving in song and color. For five days the ceremonies lasted, as they had in times long vanished, only now the people were happy. Gone were the horrors of war, slavery, hatred and bloody sacrifices, and the people felt like singing.

He organized great choruses of singers, which chanted from mountain to mountain, accompanied by orchestras of musicians. He brought in long wood and metal marimbas, pans-pipes made into four-man organs, and harps and flutes from other nations with instructors in the art of playing them, while drums of many types and sizes made up the percussion section together with conch shells, rattles and other instruments of depth and sweetness liquifying the air with music.

A tale is told of how a Captain, returning to Tula with his successful army, found instead of the usual welcome and the sacrifice of the chained captives, a peculiar disinterest in war and fighting. The captives were returned home with presents. Even the temples were strangely different.

Disgruntled, he gathered his men about him and murmured so loud at these conditions that during the evening came a summons. The Captain was escorted to the Temple.

There in the silence of the torches stood a number of white-robed figures, one of whom came forward toward him. No longer did the very walls reek of horror, but were exquisite with color and the perfumed scent of cedar. And there among them, alone save for his distant disciples, waited the Healer.

The Captain stopped and stared about him. He was no prisoner being brought to trial as indeed his men had hinted. These men were unarmed. In fact, only he, as was due his profession, carried the short sword, sharp as a razor. And only he had shield and helmet.

Yet there was something about this Person, this foreign usurping Stranger who had hypnotized the Toltecs, this man

Portion of the western range of building, Monjas, Uxmal.

they called the Feathered Serpent, Lord Over Wind and Water which protected him far more than weapons. The Captain stopped in strange confusion. And so well had he practiced his speech! So loudly had his men cheered him! This speech of anger held all his convictions, and now the words were gone, vanished like the winter snow upon the mesas.

"There is no need for you to tell me," he heard a soft, rich voice saying. "I know your thoughts, and you have your point. You fear for your country. Yet you are mistaken. You are trying to bind the infant so that it will always fit the cradle. Your enemy is not those harassed wild-tribes. Your enemy is the Law of the Jungle! Convert these people and make them happy; then there will be no need of your army."

The Captain thought bitterly of the future. With this dreamer in the temple, where would his country end? The Prophet answered in a strange language. This disciples who had been listening at a respectful distance stared at one another.

"In memory, young Macoa, I am in a tangled jungle,

120

where a little boy was clawed by a tiger. . ."

The jaw of the Captain sagged in amazement and he lifted his head and stared at the Healer with eyes puzzled and unbelieving. Then again Kate-Zahl spoke in Toltec:

"It is not this or that nation which matters. Tribes will change; they merge and mingle. To look through the eyes of the tribe is the small view. Yea, Tula will die as will Ek-Balaam. Other great nations will grow and vanish, but their blood will go on living. The jade and pearls from this very temple will someday go into jewelry for human adornment, but among the people throughout the nations my words will go on living.

"You think I seek the Bow String of Power. For what? Food? Fame? Carnal living? The first two I have never lacked. With the last, I have no interest because it is not of My Father. With the means of life, I am the teacher. The ends belong to the Almighty."

Slowly the Captain kneeled to the marble, took off his helmet, unbuckled his short swords and upon them laid his famed shield, whispering in a voice husky and awestruck:

"Forgive a mind which has been blinded. Forgive me, Oh Teo-Wahkan!"*

*This legend, told the author by several Indians with an interpreter at the site of the ruins of Teoti-huacan, I thought, because of the connection with the Guatemalan legend, so far away, authentic enough to include.

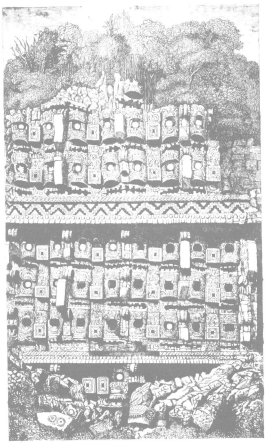

Kabah. Details of Ornament. 1st Casa.

The Coming Of The Visions

I N THE DAYS of Ancient Tula, many men were retained by the monarch to make life merry and full of nonsense in the courtyards of the Emperor. These were the men too short of stature, or hunchbacks not fit for the army. They were trained from childhood as clowns and funsters, in all the devious ways of humor. When these men came before the Prophet, He saw the tears behind their laughter and He stretched forth His hand and healed them so they were men like any other. Now no longer strange or crude of feature, they would never leave the Healer. They became His constant shadows, following Him in all His travels.

It was not long before these men realized that some great burden weighted upon their Master. Some strange, unspoken secret haunted His lonely footsteps and followed Him along the parkways. Unable to lift His spirits with laughter, they conspired with one another to probe from Him the cause of His suffering. Therefore one day in the parkways, they gathered about Him and began asking questions.

"Why do you stare at yonder bushes? Is there something there which we see not?"

"Yea, my friends. I see an earthquake. It is a very violent earthquake. Rocks are falling from the mountains. Our beautiful buildings of Tula are crumbling. My friends – I see the end of Tollan."

The clowns stared wide-eyed at the Prophet.

"Why do you not then tell the people?"

"It is far in the future, and they could not stop it."

"Are you certain they could not stop it?"

"Yea. Some of this is retribution. Perhaps I have been remiss in my teaching. . ."

"Nay, Oh Master, none could be greater."

"Then I must pray for the reason."

"When you learn of the reason, Oh Kate-Zahl, will you not then tell the people?"

"Yea. Then I shall tell the people. In the meantime, I ask that you do not tell them."

"May we ask you this: these burdensome visions, tell us how long have you had them?"

"For some time now, and they grow upon me. I can even read the dates of the cycles. Would that I could know its meaning."

"You know then the time of the earthquake?"

"Yea, it is true, I know it."

"This date - will you tell this to the people?"

"Yea. On the day when I leave Tula."

The clowns stared with eyes which were unbelieving.

"You are planning to forsake Tollan?"

"Nay, not all of the Empire. I shall make my way to Fair Co-lu-la, and from thence I must teach all of the wild tribes through many distant mountains, and someday I shall leave Fair Tollan."

"You will grieve to the soul the Toltecs, and they will never understand your leaving."

"Yea, they will see why I go teaching. I must be about My Father's Business."

"Then we shall follow you, Great Kate-Zahl."

The clowns were right about the Prophet's announcement that soon He was about to leave Tula. Strange tales were spread throughout the Empire. It was never fully understood by the Toltecs why the Prophet should wish to leave Tula - not even after He had told them about the Visions in the speech of His departure. Of course, He had often gone to the wild tribes, and on other trips through the mountains, yet He had always come back to the city. Now when He said that He was leaving forever, there was great lamentation.

Some whispered that He had been given some chocolate, or other drink that was enchanted, and which gave the imbiber a crazy desire to wander far beyond the distant horizon, because it was certain, the Toltecs argued, that no man in his right mind would forsake Tula, the Golden.

Only the clowns and the priesthood suspected the real truth, and why his shoulders always drooped with sorrow. There was one more time when the clowns pressed him, when once again they were alone in the Parkways.

"Do you still intend to tell the people?"

"Yea. In my final oration."

"Then where will you go, Master?"

"I go up into the snows of Popo, known to all men as the Smoker."

"But the ice of his hair is eternal whiteness."

"I know. But I must go alone to My Father. I must look beyond the Third Cycle."

"Then we shall follow after, Master."

"Nay. I must forbid you to follow."

Then boldly one of the funsters spoke up:

"It is beyond your power to forbid us. Whither you go, we shall follow."

"I pray that you do not go with me."

"We shall see, Beloved Master," the clowns said, smiling at one another like children who shared some mischievous secret. "We shall see when you leave Tula."

The Prophecy Of Tula

SOME SHIMMERING bits of His last oration with its strange revelations of the Future has come down to us from that bitter evening when Kate-Zahl bid farewell to his weeping Toltecs.

Usually He spoke at dawn, but this time it was almost twilight and the weather seemed to fit the mood of the moment. Many were the tears mingling with the rain-drops, many were the shoulders drooping when at the sound of the conch-shell trumpet, Kate-Zahl climbed for the last time the Hill of Loud Outcrying.

He began by naming His successor, the new Quetzal-Coatl, one of the most saintly from his priesthood. This had been known, for the ritual of ordination, of laying on of hands and of the Crown of Quetzal Feathers had been going on for days, and evenings.

Then at last, He began speaking. He told them of His deep-felt sadness, for even as He was loved here, so did He love Tula. Here the happiest hours of His lifetime had been spent with His beloved Toltecs, but a strange burden had been laid upon Him, and He could not endure its dark foreboding.

He began to speak of the Visions. They were not of the Present, but of the Future. Even Tula was becoming a nightmare.

The Toltecs gasped in consternation.

"How could Tula be a nightmare?"

He began his explanation.

Though He lived in the Present, yet did the Future press in around him. This was his real reason for leaving Tula, not the silly ones given by tongues which were wagging.

West front of the House of the Dwarf, Uxmal.

These strange visions were growing upon him. Even stronger were they among the wild tribes, driving down the reason for what He was seeing. They had to do with the Sacrificers. Ever these visions were growing upon him. Ever more clearly could He see the distance, even to the dates. Now his vision was sweeping the Third Cycle; long after the fall of Tula.

The Toltecs gasped aloud in horror.

"Nay, not by war as you are thinking. This city's end shall come with an earthquake, many generations distant. Restless drums within the mountains are the dancing Sacrificers. The Prophet Kate-Zahl is but a memory. Forgotten is Teo-Wahcan.

"Let this be a sign unto you. Closely watch Popo, the Smoker. When he seems restless, forsake your Tula, but take your books and all your learning. Have caves ready deep within the jungles. There leave them for the future ages.

"As I speak now from the Mountain and look into the Plaza of the Immortals, I see a different Golden City. The people have drifted from the One God, and strange revelries

View from La Casa de las Monjas, Uxmal, looking south.

are held in Tula. Kate-Zahl is but a name in history. Then shall come the retribution.

"With flames the mountains begin to speak! This peak where I am standing, known to men as Tza-tzi-tepec, Hill of Loud Outcrying, shall explode in fire. Then no man shall see it forever after.

"With horrible growling shall the land be shaken, furiously as the wolf does shake the rabbit. By day the light of the sun shall be darkened, and by night a new volcano shall cover the sky with comets of red fire. Down shall tumble all the temples and the walls of the houses become as rubble. Thus shall end this proud city and with it the power of Mighty Tollan.

"When the stag has fallen, the wolf pack is brave. Now shall come the Sacrificers, marching to power throughout the Broad Land. Armies shall come to Tula for plunder, but the jewels are there for the taking. Thus begins another cycle, called the Cycle of the Sacrificers.

"For awhile this was the end of Visions, but then I saw another cycle. Tonight we shall walk there together. Re-

127

Casa de los Palomos, Uxmal.

member to tell your children so that they in turn may warn
their offspring.

"Down from the north come men brandishing axes and
taking war dogs into battle. They are the first wave of many
invasions, and they are known as Chichimecas, from the
warlike dogs who go with them to battle. They are met by
the restless Serpent, the Takers of Men, the Sacrificers.
Long have I tried to teach these children, but they now turn
their heads away from my precepts. They make war, but for
the captives, as it has been from time forgotten.

"Horror shall come to the Broad Land. All shall dwell
in fear of that black-robed priesthood, who kill their captives
to feed their idols. Daily My Father's Law is broken. Hourly
do the great stones drip with fresh blood because they think
these rocks should be nourished.

"Watching this Cycle of Sacrificing is a heavy burden to
my soul. Poor, pitiful misled people. Listen carefully that
you may tell them my words after Kate-Zahl is but a
memory.

"There is a cycle beyond this one, if they do not heed

this warning. Before that cycle comes upon them, there is a man pale of feature and like unto me - bearded. Trust him not. He is not Kate-Zahl. He leads the Sacrificers into battle. He calls himself Huit-zil-po-chitli: the Bearded One Who Conquers. He shall later meet with a great warrior, and shall himself become a sacrifice to the Idol of the Tiger.

"Now the Sacrificers march to power. Go, my people, to the Jungles. Hide your treasures in the deep caves, especially the ancient histories. Most books have gone into hiding as the cycle spirals in horror, except those spared by the bloody priesthood. Learning has been conquered by the Law of the Jungle. But each day speeds the Retribution!

"Mark you well, for there shall be portents. A strange star shall cross the heavens, and all the people looking upward, as the time grows ever closer, shall remember tonight and the words of Kate-Zahl. To one another, they shall whisper: 'I fear the time has come upon us. Woe unto the Sacrificers.'

"The year is that of Te-Tec-Patl. When the dawn star, Cit-lal-pol, sometimes called Tlauiscal-Pan-Ticutli, crosses the sun for its thirteenth crossing, after the Fall of Tula, then will you know this Cycle is ended!

"That you may remember what I am saying, I have caused to be carved a giant dark boulder, highly polished and marked forever with the Dawn Star's Future Cycles. This rock has been placed in the Temple.

"Massive is the rock, and well-calculated to survive the time of earthquake and pillage far into the Time of the Future. Upon the top is the thirteenth-Acatl. Remember this date! It is the Time of Warning. With the binding date comes the retribution.*

"Stand with me in the Year of Te-Tec-Patl. Look across the Sunrise Ocean. Three ships come like great birds flying. They land. Out come men in metal garments, carrying rods which speak with thunder and kill at a distance. These men are bearded and pale of feature.

"They come ashore and I see them kneeling. Above them

(*See notes on Calendar Stone.)

129

I see a Great Cross standing. That is well. If these men are true to the symbol they carry, you need have no fear of them, for no one who is true to that symbol will ever carry it into battle.

"Therefore hold aloft your Great Cross, and go forth to meet them. They cannot fail to know that symbol, and would not fire their rods upon it, nor upon these who stand in its shadow. Well they know that what is done to my people is done also unto me."

The Prophet hesitated a moment, and then he continued more softly:

"When the years have come to their full binding, the metal tipped boots of the strangers will be heard in all the bloody temples. Then throughout the Broad Land has begun the Third Cycle. As yet, I cannot see beyond it.

"This is why I am leaving Tula. There is much work to be done among the wild tribes to turn heavy-handed destiny from them. I leave you then the most fundamental Law of My Father for your guiding life pattern: Always love one another."

"For this night, Kate-Zahl has spoken."

From the Song of Quetzal-Coatl, Bancroft; and Sedillio.

130

MEXICO

The Calendar Stone

THERE IS A mighty carved rock which is hanging in the National Museum of Mexico City. It was cut from porphyry, a volcanic stone which takes a high polish. This boulder is eleven feet across, three feet thick, and even in its present state of mutilation, it weighs twenty-four tons.

For many years after its discovery in the Eighteenth Century it was thought to be Aztec and was called the Aztec Calendar Stone. Now scientists who have studied the calendars of Mexico realize that it is far beyond the comprehension of the Aztecs, and so it is moving backward in time to the age of Tula and the Toltec Empire. The Aztecs had but a fifty-two year ritualistic calendar which is but a degenerate copy of the Toltec masterpiece of astronomical observation. In more ways than that of the calendar did the Aztecs throw the learning of Mexican civilizations back a thousand years. The Aztecs were the first conquerors to burn the ancient books, and what survived the holocaust of the Aztecs were consumed by the Spanish.

The guides at the museum are pleased to point out to the tourist the transits of the planets, the precession of the equinoxes and other marvels of learning locked up on the ancient Calendar Stone, which places it ahead of the European knowledge of its day by a millenium.

The enormous Rock of Sacrifice, now being called the Rock of the Gladiators, is also calendrical, but perhaps

131

more ancient and less understood than the Toltec Calendar Stone. That it was used for the purpose of human sacrifice by the Aztecs is unmistakable, but if one looks closely, it can be seen that the channel to carry off the blood of the

Toltec Calendar Stone.

victim was chiseled through the beautiful ancient carving. The marks about the base were made by the axes of the Spanish conquerors, who finally gave up when it broke their instruments and buried the ancient monument deep in the mud.

Once the Toltec Calendar Stone was also thought to have been buried by the Spanish. However, the Indians now tell a far more comprehensive story which is gaining precedence, as more and more full-blooded Indians in Mexico take their doctorates in various branches of archaeology and anthropology.

The Toltec Calendar Stone, having been taken from ravaged Tula first by the Chichimecas and then in turn by the Aztecs, was placed in the Aztec temple in Tenoch-titlan (Mexico City) so that the carved face stood outward where the people could see it. If they had fully understood what they were doing, they might not have done so. As it was, the people watched with ever-increasing apprehension the approach of the Time of Warning, which was the uppermost glyph, apparently a large aloe like the maguey plant (the sacred plant of the Aztecs), and about it as well as the container which held it were thirteen circles representing stars.

As the time approached, near panic took place in all the land, so the Emperor, Mocte-zoma, had a new, smaller calendar stone made without a date of warning, and buried the original deeply under the mud of the streets. Thus he thought to banish the threat to his throne and empire predicted so long before. It becomes increasingly evident that if the Aztecs had understood this calendar and its predictions, they would not have placed it in their main temple in the first place.

Nevertheless, the people had not forgotten the Toltec Calendar Stone, and when the first two centuries of the Conquest had passed, the Calendar Stone was again dug up and returned to its present place of honor in the National Museum where it covers most of the great blank wall facing the entrance, so that it is the first sight to greet the visitor.

There is another idea expressed by Leon Y. Gama who saw the "Dark Rock" when it was first uncovered. Noting that the circle of carving does not exactly correspond to the square, he theorized that there was another "cycle" or companion piece. Probably this was the earlier "First Cycle" or the time following the Conquest, which would include the present? Were there more cycles than these?

Bancroft, writing about a century after Gama, notes that no systematic search for ancient monuments such as these two mentioned, i.e. the Toltec Calendar Stone and the Altar of the Gladiators has ever been made. Furthermore, some sculptured blocks of the greatest scientific value have actually been seen while excavating for large buildings, but they have again been covered up and allowed to remain undisturbed under the pavements and public parks of a great modern metropolis.

Incidentally, speaking of the Toltec Calendar Stone, Cortez arrived in the year Te-Tec-Patl as prophesied so long before in Tula by the Prophet.

MEXICO

Legend Of The Pass Of Popocatepetl

THROUGH A MIST of dancing snowflakes moved a lonely figure dressed in a long, white mantle. All about were moving snowflakes like a shower of flying sea-foam, covering everything with silver. The bared head of the man was crested with whiteness. His beard and lashes were stiff with hoar-frost. He moved slowly, then staggered against a ledge of darkened lava, lightly brushed with the dust of snowflakes. There He slumped and rested, kneeling.

Suddenly the darkness of the heavens was split with a blinding bolt of lightning. With its flash the man could see the valley, and sobbing, His head fell forward. His cold lips moved out a silent prayer:

"Take me to they bosom, Father. I have seen enough. I am weary and sick with the visions of the future. Cover me with thy mantle and leave my body here on Popo - on Popo, the Mighty Smoker."

Then a strange miracle happened.

The storm clouds parted, and in the magnificent rays of the sun the man looked downward at a Vision. Lit by a shaft of golden sunlight was a city in the valley, and the man straightened, watching, His hands pressed upon the dark ledge, while He stared in awe and wonder.

Today, in the vale of Teme-palco, high in the snowy pass or Popo, the natives say there is a rock ledge where at times one can see a strange sight. There is an imprint of hands in the lava and the curve of a body sagging as if one had knelt there in anguish and had stared backward toward Tula.

The Tree Of The Lightning

TO QUAH-AH-TITLAN also came the Healer, past an ancient ruined city. No one seemed to know of its history, and the Prophet wandered onward to a giant tree beneath whose branches the Plumed Serpent rested.

As the people pressed around Him, the Prophet seemed quiet and weary.

"If you cannot remember your ancient cities, then how can you remember all the precepts which I have taught you? Can you retain them through the future; through the coming Dawn Star cycles? Or must you return to the Sacrificers?"

"We shall never forget you, Master."

Kate-Zahl smiled. Then a woman pushed forward, holding closely a crying baby.

"Oh, please say that you will hold my baby."

He shook his head slowly and sadly.

"I have lost my power. Now I am a man like any other."

From the people there were cries of unbelief. He held aloft his hand for quiet.

"Sit down and I will tell a story."

On the grass, they gathered around Him.

"There walked one time in the streets of Tula a man who could see the Future. It pressed in upon him from the parkways, from the temples and the happy people. Finally he was impelled to leave the city. He must go into the highest mountain and there try to reach the Great Spirit. Of what use were these years of teaching a Peace Religion when the Fu-

Mitla.

ture was so filled with warfare? When would there be an end to this carnage?

"Yet, when he tried to leave the city those who had been dwarfs and hunchbacks whom he had healed would not forsake him. He pleaded and argued, but they would not leave him, and like disobedient children they still followed at a distance.

"Far up in the snows which are eternal came the blinding, choking blizzard. In massive choruses came the snowflakes; with howling chanting came the ice-wind, and crossing through, more snowflake dancers.

"The man turned, and then he saw the jesters. They had huddled together in a snow bank, looking toward him with eyes which were frozen. He returned and could not warm them. Into hard ice the jesters had become, and his hands could in no wise move them.

"The soul of the man was crushed with sorrow. Now he knew that he had lost favor. He wandered on to the Pass of Popo, praying for the Great Spirit to take him.

"The answer came with a crash of lightning, and then a shaft of dazzling sunlight. For the first time he saw beyond the Visions. Thus he came back down the mountain, but his power was left behind with the jesters, hard and cold in the snows of Popo."

136

Kabah, third Casa.

"Great Kate-Zahl," pleaded the woman, "please hold my baby. Hold him up against your mantle."

"But I no longer have the power to heal him or stop his crying if that crying is due to illness."

"Nay. His limbs are withered."

"Poor lamb. I should like to heal him, but now I am as any other."

"I care not if you cannot heal him. I only ask that in the days which are coming, he may say to the people that once he was held by Kate-Zahl."

With a smile the Prophet consented, and lifted the infant to his shoulder. Then a laughing child ran up with a bow and arrow which he aimed above the head of the Healer, toward the bark of the forest giant. Kate-Zahl turned to seize the arrow even as it struck the tree trunk and a blinding flash came from the Heavens. When the people could again look upward, they saw the Prophet staring at the great tree trunk, for carved deep in its bark-coat was the Giant Cross, symbol of Kate-Zahl, and the Great Spirit.

When the people saw this miracle they were astonished,

Xampon.

but yet another miracle awaited them, for as the Healer
turned to hand back the laughing baby, its limbs were
straight and its body was sturdy. Then as one the People fell
down, whispering to one another:

"He is indeed the Son of the Spirit. He is still Kate-Zahl,
the Mighty."

Yet the Prophet saw that they stared at him strangely,
and so he asked for an obsidian mirror. When he looked
therein, he saw the reason.

No longer he saw there the Prophet of Tula. The features
which stared back at him from the mirror were framed with
hair as white as snowflakes, and the beard was as pale as the
hoar-frost of Popo. The eyes beneath their brows of silver,
still turquoise green as ocean shadows, held a wisdom
greater than those which bade farewell to Tula, and there
was a deeper peace about them.

But the people, looking with love upon him, whispered to
one another: "How well the snows of Popo become the frame
for His lofty features. He is more a god than ever: the
Magnificent Pale One! Radiant Kate-Zahl."

138

Is the Tree of the Lightning still alive? Perhaps. It may be the arboreal giant whose arms shelter the plaza of a small town in Me-She-Co, but whose crippled trunk bears the axe-marks of hatred. Unfortunately, Cortez the Conqueror stopped here one night when he thought his army defeated. Since then, so violently has Cortez been hated that a high iron fence has had to be built about the ancient monarch, to protect the tree from the wrath of the people.

Yet if you stop close to the giant and look lovingly upward through its branches, you will see the Great Cross of the Tree of Lightning. The wind which sings through it seems to whisper:

"I was aged when the Toltec armies passed here on their way to Tula. Here also have other conquerors rested - even before the rise of the Toltecs.

"For rich and for poor has my shade been poured forth, but once there was a day which was different. He came here in a snow-white mantle. He leaned on my bark and told the people about His terrible night on Popo the Smoker. It was here He discovered that His hair had turned white, even as it was on top of the mountain, and did remain so ever after. It was here that He took the crying infant, believing His power had gone forever, but that power was restored in a crash of lightning which burned on me His living symbol to go on down throughout the ages."

When the earth has entered another cycle, and the scars of the Spanish Conquest are gone, restore, oh people of Ancient Me-She-Co, the Toltec name to this aged monarch, living on down through Time's long cycles. Call it once more "Sacred Tree of the Lightning" and remember when you do so that it is sacred: this living thing once touched by the Prophet.

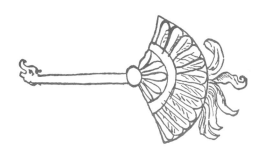

The Legend Of Colula

COLULA WAS called the Sacred City, for it was towered with many temples; as many as there were days in the Sun Year. This was the Second City of Mighty Tollan, and greatly beloved was the Plumed Serpent, the Fair God of Wind and Water. Here Kate-Zahl came and constructed His greatest temple, the mighty pyramid of Quetzal-Coatl, with a greater base than Egypt's Cheops. There is a legend that it was begun by Xelhua the Thunderer after the flood of the Destruction. However, it was finished by the Healer. Legends say it was fashioned of stone blocks, but Kate-Zahl covered its sides with metal, gold and jewel encrusted until it shimmered in exquisite beauty. When the sunlight fell upon it, the glow was as from a thousand million mirrors. Yet loveliest of all was the Temple by torchlight when the dancers moved upon it during the nights of festival dancing.

Like Tula, here too were the Toltec Parkways, wire-netted and filled with feathered singers; here too the vast maze of markets, and the wide, white city of the people.

In the Great Temple, the Plumed Serpent fashioned the Hall of the Four Directions. To the east was the golden room of the Sunrise; to the north the crimson of the flame-curtains which drop down from the skies in winter; to the west the blue of the Sunset Ocean mosaiced in turquoise and emerald with the bluish irridescence of the Xiuhtotl; while in the south, for the snows of the Far Lands, this room was finished in pearl and silver with the frost-like beauty of delicate feathers.

Here the Prophet blessed the children, the seeds ready for the planting, and the animals belonging to the farmers.

Gone today is its ancient beauty. The Aztecs, when they came to power, did not bow to Quetzal-Coatl. They did not touch His Pyramid, but they committed the subtle heresy of killing men on the sacred altars to fend off

Quetzal Coatl Pyramid at Teotihuacan.

141

the time of retribution. They could not forget His predictions, and with blood they tried to woo Him. With fear and awe they looked on His Temple.

This was not true of the Spanish. The bloodiest battle of all Meshico was fought over the Sacred City. From tier to tier up the Great Pyramid the battle was fought, and when the Spanish finally reached the summit and had killed all the defenders, they were amazed to see a statue worked in pale marble of a Christ-like man in a flowing mantle standing with outstretched arms to greet them.

Furious at what they considered mockery they set upon the statue with their bloody hatchets, smashing it into a glittering rock-pile. Then they turned to plundering the Temple. First they tried to destroy the Pyramid as they had the statue. With whips they drove the suffering people and told them to tear down the "Sacred Mountain", but the people would rather be killed than deface the old shrine. So the Spanish had to be contented with making their slaves carry up much mud to pour over the monument. The other temples were turned into churches, but the people ignored them.

Very surprising to the conquerors was the way of the people. Even in the rain they trudged up the Great Hill, kneeling and weeping upon the summit. Hither they brought their sick and injured. Here they carried fruits and seeds for the harvest and the few animals which had been left to them.

Seeing this odd veneration, the Spanish constructed a church on the summit and placed therein a statue of the Virgin, calling it the Chapel of Healing, on the spot where once stood an ancient altar.

So today the people stream upward, laying gifts before the Pale Virgin, and as they cross themselves with an ancient symbol, some think but of the moment, but there are some whose thoughts move backward to a day when the Plumed Serpent stood here, and gently to their fathers pronounced His blessing.*

(*Legend from Sedillio,
Bancroft and Mayans.)

142

MEXICO

The Grove At Tule

IN THE DAYS of the Prophet there lived, as today it is still living, an aged cedar in the Grove of Tule, in the state called Wah-ha-ca (Oaxaca). For time beyond the history of nations this tree has been an object of worship. It has lived through wars and times of famine. Nations have been born and flourished to greatness, been conquered and turned back to rubble, yet the great cedar has gone on living.

Some said that it was planted by Votan, with the seeds he brought from the Old Red Land which sank below the Sunrise Ocean; and others said it had been called into being by· another monarch of forgotten antiquity: namely Tohil the Thunderer. No one knows for certain.

When Kate-Zahl first saw its massive proportions, He ordered a temple to be built near it and called it the "Tree of our Father", saying to the people who gathered around Him: "Remember to protect this giant always, for it is the oldest thing that is living upon the entire face of our planet."

It was there that He watched the Zapotecas dance their Calendar Dance of the Feathers. And as He watched, sometimes by moonlight, He leaned against a younger cedar. Thus the Zapotecas named the trees the Tree of Our Father and the Tree of the Pale Son.

143

Base of trunk of Giant Cedar of Tule, called "The Tree of the Father" for ages.

Twenty-five men, arms outstretched and fingers touching, barely encircle this giant.

Garbed in their costumes of pearl and emerald, in nodding gossamer plumes of metal, with costumes of the finest seed-silk and topped with rare and exquisite feathers, this dance was a sight of rhythmical beauty. Since the happy days of Kate-Zahl, conquest has taken the exquisite costumes, the pride and wealth of the Zapotec people, and today they dance in paper headdress.

Yet it is whispered in Wah-ha-ca, when the moon is of pale silver and the leaves of the trees are falling, that if no one is watching but the faithful then the costumes become rare jewels, and the paper changes to the most exquisite featherwork with nodding, irridescent quetzal feathers.

Nor is this all, for on rare occasions a figure dressed in a long white toga with black crosses embroidered about the hemline and hair like the misty pearl of the moonlight leans against the Tree of the Pale Son and raises His hand in benediction.*

(*An Oaxaca Legend.)

The Legends Of Travel

O N THE HIGH mountain crest of Wah-ha-ca (Oaxaca), Mexico, is the ruins of a city extending along the mountain ridge. Tourists standing on the ruins of the pyramids and buildings now being excavated from the rubble of ages see the rain water of the storm vanish through the ancient sewers which have not yet been completely uncovered.

Here are to be seen strange rock carvings. One seems to be the court of an Egyptian Pharaoh, and near it is a great ape of Africa, beating its breast and screeching. There are others equally puzzling: apparently a figure of ancient China, and a negro. Here during the excavations was found, along with the exquisite gold work similar to the master-smiths or jewelers of ancient Chan-Chan, Peru, a Peruvian vase of the typical Nasca cat-faced design. Both the Nasca Empire, and that of Chan-Chan were overwhelmed by the rise of the Incas, and before their extinction were great trading Empires.

This ancient city of Wah-ha-ca, (whose ruins run 24 miles long) today renamed Monte Alban, according to carbon-dating was sacked and burned about 750 AD. which could tell us that the Peruvian Empires were also living before this dateline, for almost anywhere in the world, among those who follow archaeology, the vase of one nation found among the treasures of another, means trade.

If one rules out trade, then there are many puzzles. Who carried the gourd, the yam and the pineapple back and forth from the Americas to the South Sea Islands? What ships bore the banana, or American corn to the far-off Philippines, both plants which must be planted? Throughout the tropics the lists are endless. The trees from which the Polynesians get their war-clubs and those from which they make their bark-cloth are to be found in Brazil's Matto Grosso, and the natives there make bark-cloth with the same beaters in identical fashion.

Among the people are trading legends, and on the ships of the traders rode the Prophet. All the merchants wished to have Him for He had a magical power over the ocean. Perhaps it was while in Colula that He rode to the South American cities, but we know not yet whose ships carried Him, whether those of Mayans, Toltecs or the Zapotecans who lived in beautiful Monte Alban. Or again, perhaps He rode with the returning Peruvians? Perhaps He spent years on these journeys, before again coming home to Sacred Co-lu-la.

We only know that we can trace Him throughout the lands of South America, not only by His Wakea names when His hair was light brown with its reddish highlights, but also with names as different as the tribes who remember, and with hair as white as the snows of winter. Sometimes as Tama, or Cama or Caboy they speak of Him, and sometimes as Sume or Vira-Cocha. Yet the descriptions always tally. He wears His white mantle with the crosses at the hem-line, and His feet are shod in golden sandals.

They always remember His hands which were healing, His hatred of war and of sacrificing. They know the Peace Sign of His religion, and often speak of His control of the water and how He walked at will on its surface.

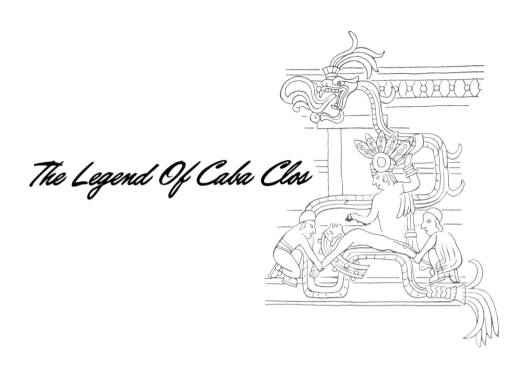

The Legend Of Caba Clos

THE CITY of Caba Clos first saw the Pale God when He stopped the tempest and jelled the sea for His ship's landing, then easily walked across the waters. They remembered His strange magnetism for before Him the fiercest animals lay down and allowed Him to caress them.

For His One God, the Divine Spirit, they built a temple. Then He left them to teach other nations, promising to return to dedicate the temple.

Alas for man and his jealous priesthood. The Sacrificers were again in power when once more the Pale God, Sume, returned. The priests had busily told the people that this was a demon who had bewitched tnem. Accordingly when Sume returned along the highway in His long white mantle and His great staff, keeping His promise to the people to dedicate His temple, warriors lay in wait behind the bushes, their arrows already strung in their long-bows.

The puzzled people, led by the black-robed Sacrificers came forward. Then at a signal from the Head priest the warriors sprang out of the foliage and a rain of arrows went toward the Prophet.

Standing atop a slight mound, Sume raised His palms high over His head and called aloud in a foreign language.

Then a curious miracle happened. A curtain of flame, fiercely whirling, came down upon Him from the heavens, clear up to now with a bright sun shining. This curtain circled all about the Healer. The arrows of the Caba-Clos warriors could not penetrate the curtain. They glanced off as if from hard rock and struck again through the bows which had sent them, burying their shafts deep in the breasts of the senders.

When the people saw this they were stricken with terror, and the priesthood fell down sobbing.

In the center of the curtain Sume stood waiting, and when it lifted He turned his back upon them and walked away sadly along the seashore. His footsteps were pressed deeply in the wet sand, where none have ever been able to erase them.

Even today, along the Caba-Clos River, one can still see the steps of Sume, the Fair God as He walked away from the wicked city.*

(*Legend repeated by Bancroft from "Recherchez", by Warden, not (apparently) obtainable today.)

The Legend Of
The Three Crosses

THE GOLDEN sandals of the Prophet came to Paracas in Peru, South America. As in the land now called Mexico (Place of the Meshecans) when He went toward Tula, His coming was announced by trumpeteers sounding the conch-shells and drummers talking with the tom-toms. For three hundred miles from mountain to mountain, in all the four directions, the great news travelled.

Also as in the north, the tribesmen answered. Like a flood of churning waters came the people. Down from every mountain hamlet, up from every larger village, along each stream in their ships of balsa (that light-weight wood which floats like a dry leaf), from every direction came the people.

On a hillside facing the Bay of Paracas stood the Healer, looking down on the surging thousands. The sun shone bright on His mantle of seed-silk as He held His arm aloft for silence, giving the sign they knew was His Peace Sign. The people stilled, expectantly waiting.

Then from the earth came the terrible rumble which comes before the roar of the Fire God, and the earth began to sway and shake beneath them. The people, frightened, clung together, staring wide-eyed at one another, trying to silence their crying children. In their eyes were unspoken questions.

Was the Fire God who dwells in the lava, the red-blood of the earth, Ah Musem-Cab, showing his anger at this Lord of Wind and Water?

"Why was he roaring if not in anger?"

Only the Pale One stood there silent, unmoved by all the earth-shaking, His arm still raised in benediction. Finally silence came to the people.

"Fear not, my children. My Father, who rules the earth

149

Ancient Building with Cross, Island of Mugeres.

and the heavens, is not showing His anger. He but shakes the earth to prick my memory. He reminds me that I have a story to tell you.''

Then the Prophet began a strange story, yet He told it so well, with such vivid detail, that each man felt He had once been a witness, and the silence was so thick one could hear it.

He told them of a land across the ocean, where all men were like Him: bearded. He spoke of their houses, their cattle, their clothes and customs, their ships and temples, their metal-clad armies.

Then He spoke of a Man who had lived there, who healed the people, who taught them and loved them, and in turn was beloved of the people. Yet this Man incurred in the priest-hood jealousy and anger which ran like a bad sore, corrupting even those who should have known better.

He spoke of the power of a wicked nation who bowed down before many idols. Into a court of this nation the Man was dragged by His captors. Even the judge could see no wrong in Him, but as His enemies called furiously for His

150

Zayi.

life, the judge was forced at last to condemn the Prisoner
to be hung upon a cross of dead trees - for such was their
strange custom.

In prison, the Man had been lashed and beaten, and when
the day arrived for execution, the Prisoner had to carry
His great cross to a place upon a hilltop, falling down often
upon the hot earth, for He was weak from His stay in
prison. Some there were who tried to help Him. Yet there
were many who cried out against Him with curses that showed
their livid hatred, while spit mingled with His bloody bowed
head. Thus He dragged His cross to a hilltop.

To each side, and a little behind Him, two thieves were
fastened to crosses, and then the soldiers made Him fast to
the big cross by driving knives through His two hands and
raising up the dead trees so that He would hang there until
death at last had released Him.

These thieves cried out to Him for a benediction. They
were of good heart, even though they had done wrong.
Compared to those who had tried to spread hatred, and from
their own little self-minded islands were attempting to

151

Yalahao.

stamp Him with their own evil which corrupted their souls like a sore over-running, these thieves were good and so He blessed them.

Then He asked for a drink, as the pain hung on Him, and at last as His head fell forward, He asked forgiveness for all who had wronged Him.

No sooner had this happened than the earth began heaving. The sun was darkened and the people ran screaming. The three figures swung to and fro on their crosses and a fierce wind swept over the hilltop.

Then seeing that He was apparently lifeless, the soldiers brought down the great cross, and a man who had been His friend came forward to claim Him.

This man was wealthy, being the owner of ships which carried goods to the four directions on both of the oceans. He had bought a tomb for the humble Healer, because he believed his Peace Religion. To this tomb was the Man carried, where He was tended with loving care and laid in a casket. A great rock was rolled against the entrance, lest some try to do Him further evil.

152

Larphak.

Yet when the women came there weeping, behold the stone had been rolled away and the tomb was empty. For a few short days, some said that they had seen Him and then He was seen no more.

"Thus my children, does the Almighty protect the Man who carries his message, and not even one of the earth's greatest nations in all its might has the power to kill Him while He follows the wishes of the Almighty.

"So too, is it with Me. And when just now the earth started shaking, it was to remind Me of this story which My Father had laid upon my heart to tell you so that you many know more about this Peace Religion."

It is said that when He finished speaking, the people could see behind Him upon the hillside the shadow of three crosses.

After He had gone, the people still seemed to see three crosses, so stone-masons began the work of carving them deeper upon the hillside so that the children of their children would still remember.

Today, if you go to the Bay of Paracas and look across

at the hillside, you may still see the Three Crosses. The Great Cross in the center is six hundred feet tall, while the smaller two are to each side of the Great Cross. There is a line which ties each of the smaller crosses to the Great Cross.

These huge carvings are indeed strange crosses. They resemble dead trees with limbs turned upward, like arms raised in supplication.

Scientists stare at them in utter amazement. Solemnly they admit their antiquity. These works probably date from the Age of Jesus. But the meaning? That escapes these men who are learned. They can only shake their heads in wonder. The meaning is beyond their understanding.

Indian Priest.

(Note: The Legend of the Three Crosses and the Waters of Vira Cocha were told me by a native Indian of Peru who was laughingly introduced to me by a Navaho friend as a Navaho. No one would have guessed that he was not until he admitted being a Quichua. I was grateful for the legends, but I am unable to find them in print either in Bancroft or other authorities. However, they do seem very probable, so I am including them. The described works in both cases are authentic. The line of the crosses is true North-South - Author.)

154

Gigantic head at Izamal.

The Legend Of
The City Of Cocha

BY NOW the Healer was very famous, but it seemed His visits ended with the unhappy one to Cocha. Here the Sacrificing Priesthood had a strong seat of power. On His first visit they did not oppose Him, knowing that a ship was waiting for Him, but the building of a temple and a promise to dedicate it became a gnawing worry because of His hold upon the people. The priesthood feared a revolution, and so when news came by obsidian mirrors that the Pale God was returning, the Priesthood decided to kill Him.

They had heard about the disaster at Caba Clos, but they chose to disbelieve it, and so changed the story that the army was willing to surround Him and exterminate this demon. Therefore careful were the plans they laid out, and with great care was the strategy followed.

First, the Priesthood lectured the people. "This could not be Vira Cocha, a hero of the most ancient legends. This man was an imposter. He was a demon who had ensnared their reason. He was a devil who wished to turn them from the worship of their ancestral idols. Too long bloodless had been the temples! If the people would not feed them, their ancestral idols would fade away to nothing and with them the greatness of the people. This man must die!"

The army, listening, agreed that this creature was an imposter with no greater power than any other. Very well, they would kill Him and rid the land of His evil power.

As the Prophet approached the city, the army drew its lines before the people and pushed them back from the highway.

From a distance, the Prophet saw this, and the forward

156

Portion of western building, Monjas, Uxmal.

march of the black-robed priesthood. He stopped and climbed upon a small mound, and raised His arm high in greeting.

Suddenly the army gave its answer. With the mighty yell of battle they brandished their spears and started for Him, while behind them the Sacrificers, picking up rocks and hurling them at Him, called loudly in tones of derision:

"You pretend to have power - then display it! Save yourself if you are able!"

For a moment the Prophet hesitated, seeing some of the people weeping, then He knelt upon the small mound and cried aloud so that all could hear Him:

"Oh, My Father, who art in Heaven, if it be thy will now to take me, and this be the manner - I am ready."

Suddenly the clear air was split with lightning! From out of nowhere came the fire-flame! Making a ring about the Prophet, it whirled about in magnificent color.

The army and the priesthood began to panic, turning about to run backward. A second curtain formed behind them, separating them from the people. Here they were trapped in a sheet of horror which dissolved them into fine blown ashes before the shocked eyes of the watchers. The curtains died down and a terrible quiet left every man without the will of movement.

Now the people fell down on their faces, seeing the white robe of the Healer was not even singed by the blue-hot fire-flame. Then a deep voice came in the thunder, rumbling down from the heavens, speaking the words of a foreign language which somehow were simultaneously translated for the people so that they clearly understood the meaning:

"Go, my Son, upon thy journey, for thy work in this land is ended."

Then the Prophet turned and walked away sadly toward the bay where His ship had been waiting.

Now the people, ashamed and grieving, followed Him at a distance as He walked on toward the ocean. Through the afternoon and into the evening, He passed through the province of Canas, not stopping until He reached the seashore. There in the moonlight, holding His robe close about Him, He began treading the trail of moonbeams over the quiet shine of the water to where His great ship was riding.

Now the people fell down weeping, saying: "It was Vira Cocha, returned to us from the land of the Shadows, and we, his people, did not know him."*

Today if you should go to Peru, and visit the City of Cocha, find an old man who knows the legends and ask him to take you to the Place of the Lightnings.

There circled about a small mound you will see the strange rocks near an old road which the people say were formed on a clear day when an early sun was shining. So light are these rocks that a table-sized boulder can be balanced on the back of one hand. So hot was the fire that formed them.

(*For this Legend see Bancroft. By using this legend as a wedge, quoting a Quichua Indian from Peru, I learned the following Legend of the Fountain of Vira Cocha, which is its sequel. - Author.)

The Temple of the Dead at Mitla.

The Waters Of Vira Cocha

AFTER THE PROPHET had gone from Cocha and walked away on the trail of the Moonlight, the people began to retrace their footsteps. Wearily they camped for the night on a mesa, and then during the early morning began their long return to their city with its vanished priesthood and its unfinished temple.

Sad indeed was this walk of the people. They kept saying to one another:

"Why, oh why, did we not know Him?"

"Why did we listen to the priesthood?"

"Why did we let the army surround Him?"

To these questions they had no answer, but they urged their crying children onward, and dragged their tired feet homeward.

Then came the great disappointment.

The Apurimac River, never known to lessen the flow of its clear water, was dry! The people of Cocha were stricken. This was the displeasure of the Great Spirit! What would they do for water? Dismayed and distracted were the people, and seeing their parent's confusion, the children were doubly distracted.

They held a meeting and spoke of many plans. The wisest argued to keep on walking toward Cocha. If death waited for the people, why not near their own city?

Yet as they came near the Place of Lightnings, they broke into lamentation. Spirits crushed, they huddled together. All the springs were dried and dusty, all the small streams were empty. Truly now they knew that they had offended, for each dry spring was an added witness to the wrath of the Almighty.

160

Collossal serpent heads, Yucatan.

That night the people chanted together; an olden chant from days long-vanished. It was the fourth night of their long penance, and they had little hope for forgiveness or continuing life. Upon some of them had come the thirst-madness, and four had died for want of water. Most desperately the little children suffered. Now in their chant they asked not for forgiveness, but only for help for their suffering children.

Suddenly in the east rose the Star of the Dawning - and a luminous Being stood among them. His hair and beard, touched by the moonlight, were rippling streams of burnished silver, and His white robe seemed to be made of moonbeams. In one hand He grasped a long staff. This He raised and thrust deep into the lava. A fountain of water sprang up, bubbling and tumbling its way among them.

In a moment they had fallen into it, soaking the water into their garments, crying and laughing as they felt it splash over them, carrying hither their shrunken babies. Cool water! It brought life to a dying people.

Then the people thought to thank Him but He was not there. He was gone - as much as if He had been but a dream of the imagination. Yet the water was there, splashing, singing, shining its way through the fields of lava. They called it the Fountain of Vira Cocha.

Some say to this day that perhaps His returning was but a dream of the thirst-madness. Yet most of the people only say that His great staff brought the water of life to a dying people, and in all Peru no stream is more holy than the sacred Fountain of Vira Cocha.

Through the ages from that day this spring has been worshipped. Here came the mighty Inca, ruler of a hundred nations. Here, where the waters reach a depression, the monarch had a large dam constructed so that a blue lake would sparkle, filled with the sacred water.

About this lake was a wall of great stones, eight feet high and six in width, and at one end a giant structure. For some three hundred feet ran this temple, its breadth eighty seven feet, its walls in tiers of twenty feet each, rising twelve tiers with many windows which had wooden sashes. Six courtyards stood before the temple, each surrounded by

Rain symbol.

six buildings, two on each of three sides leaving the fourth side open to the lake. These buildings were made of unhewn lava, with well fitted windows, all well cemented, the second story of stucco and painted purple.

Beyond these buildings were others, some of circular stones, and beyond these walls were still other buildings.

Above the courtyards stood a giant statue of Vira Cocha seen and described by the Spaniard, Garcilasso. The statue was of a man very lofty of feature, with long curling hair and a flowing beard. He was dressed in a cassock, not unlike those of Biblical times, and behind Him walked a chained tiger.

Gone today are the buildings with the slanting roofs and the Statue of the Prophet. Only ruins remain of the lovely temple, but if you should go to the River Vilcanota, flowing between Cuzco and Lake Titicaca, you may find the town of Cacha, which once was known as Cocha. Beyond the town, on the right bank of the river, near the volcano of Haratche, is the Sacred Spring of Vira Cocha, splashing its way in gurgling music through the lava to a large artificial lake.

This is the most sacred spring in South America, the life-giving Waters of Vira Cocha where the Prophet once stood and thrust His staff into the lava to save a repentant nation from death.*

Sunrise, Dawn.

(*For Garcillasso's description (now lost), see George E. Squier's "Peru", (also very difficult to obtain), quoted by Bancroft.)

The Coming Of The Strangers

MEXICO

EVERYONE HAD seen the strangers. From the markets to the parkways, from the fountains to the rooftops, everywhere the news had travelled. For days the people had watched the Temple for a glimpse of the bearded strangers.

Led by a delegation of the lordly Itzaes, they had come into the city, and the people were amazed. These men were dressed much like the Prophet, except that their robes were made in color. The Toltecs stared at the strangers. These men were, like the Healer, bearded, yet on their heads they wore a mantle. Otherwise, they were like Kate-Zahl, although their features were not as lofty.

It was whispered that when they were led to the Temple, the Great One looked with favor on them and embraced one like a long-lost brother. This one brought with him a message: a hide upon which marks had been written. It had been rolled about a stick and tied securely. The Prophet took it, unrolled it and read. Something therein seemed to make make Him happy, or at least it gave Him pleasure, for long these men spoke with the Pale One in some strange foreign language which not even the best translators among the Toltecs could fathom. The Itzaes looked equally puzzled.

For four days the strangers remained. Then when came the dawn of the day of parting, Kate-Zahl said farewell on the steps of the Temple. Yet it was such a happy parting that the people, watching, wondered.

"He did not leave," the Toltecs murmured to one another. "He must be planning to remain with us."

"But not for long," whispered the doubters. "See how joyful is the parting? This can only mean one thing for Fair Colula; there will come a day of farewell, and then as He left Tula, the Plumed Serpent will also leave us."

After the strangers had left with the Itzaes, much more was learned about them. As everyone knew, the Itzae cities were spread along the Sunrise Ocean. From those who had met these men in the markets, or strolling along the parkways, the people heard more about the strangers. The bearded ones had come in a vessel, much like a bird which is flying, for it had white outstretched wings which did propel it rapidly across the water, although there was also room for many rowers. Bound by rope against the long quay, the great vessel was waiting to accept once more its wandering cargo.

Unhappily the people watched the calendar. Well-known was the fact that the Feathered Serpent never left a well-loved city except at the time of New Year's observance. Not distant was that celebration.

The ultimate signs of His departure began to crowd upon them. He had chosen one of the Priesthood (from the favored Twelve who were always around Him) to be His successor. This was a saintly man whom the others respected. Then another was chosen to take his vacancy, for the Prophet always left a Saintly twelve about the new Quetzal-Coatl. Was thirteen not His number?

Next came the public ceremonials. It is said that the

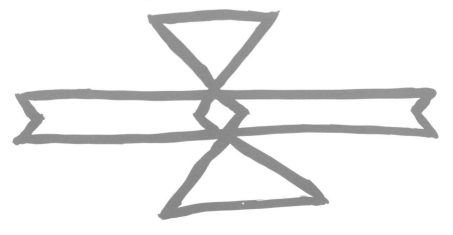

Mesa, or mountains.

165

appointed had been given instructions, and now he was to be ordained as leader, and the Crown of the Plumed Serpent placed on his forehead. Yet the most sacred of all ceremonies was when the Prophet placed His hands on the kneeling man's shoulders, and then the Crown of Office upon his shoulders.

Now there was a new Quetzal-Coatl.

For the people it was an hour of sadness. As the days had approached the time of One Reed, the Great One had announced His departure. He was going to the Sunrise Ocean. There He would teach the many nations of the Mayan-speaking peoples. However His days would be numbered. He had made an appointment in Tla-Pallan, where a great council awaited Him bearing news of more distant people.

A vessel would come one day to take Him. It would tie up at Cosmul, a seaport filled with long-docks for the larger vessels. This ship would carry Him eastward toward the land where the Sun is Rising, known to men as Tla-Pallan. Long had men known of this Great Island, but it took two years to make the journey and return. The ships always returned with strange oils, spices, wild animal skins and other treasures not known here in all the Broad Land.

The people grieved to hear this.

"Wilt thou ever return, oh much-loved Master?"

"Yea, in times more distant, I shall return to all the Broad Land, for greatly indeed do I love thee."

Thus a promise had been given, and Kate-Zahl never broke a promise.

So the Toltecs sat through the ceremonies, sad at heart with eyes which were weeping. Only one thing more was there for the people. That was the Prophet's farewell message.

MEXICO

The Prophecy At Co Lula

WHEN THE Prophet climbed His Temple in the beautiful morning of One Reed, the Toltecs were weeping for now they knew that He was leaving, and perhaps never again through the ages would He walk the Toltec Empire.

Once more He took them through the cycles of the Dawn Star, sometimes called the Star of the Prophet, Tlau-Iacal-Pan-Tecutli, and into the vistas of the Future.

He repeated the warning given at Tula against the deeds of the Sacrificers, and foretold the invasion of White Man. He repeated again the description: the suits of shining metal, the rods which make much noise and kill at a distance.

Then He bowed His head in silence. When again He began, it seemed to the people that His voice was husky with teardrops.

"Once I had great hope for these people, for I saw them kneel and kiss the sweet earth, and I saw the shadow of the Great Cross which they carried with them. Yea, I had great faith in these people. Now I must warn you against them.

"Carry your great books into the jungles. Place your histories deeply in caverns where none of these men can find them. Nor do you bring them back to the sunlight until the War-Cycle is over. For children of War are these bearded strangers. They speak my precepts, but their ears do not listen. They follow only the Law of the Jungle. They seek naught but the golden metal as if that would buy them passage into the Isles of the Blessed.

"They have but one love and that is for weapons. Ever more horrible are these weapons, until they reach for the one which is ultimate. Should they use that, there will be no forgiveness in that vale where there is no turning. Using such a weapon to make man over, is reaching into space for the God-Head. These things are not for man's decision, nor should man presume to think for all things, and thus hurl mockery at the Almighty. Woe to those who do not listen! There are lamps beyond that which you are burning; roads beyond this which you are treading; worlds beyond the one you are seeing. Be humble before the might of the Great Hand which guides the stars within their places. There are many lodges in My Father's Kingdom for it is more vast than Time, and more eternal.

"Keep hidden your books, oh my children, all during the Cycle of Warring Strangers. The day will come when they will be precious."

"For five full Cycles of the Dawn Star, the rule of the warring strangers will go on to greater and greater orgies of destruction. Hark well to all I have taught you. Return not to the Sacrificers. Their path will lead to the Last Destruction. Know that the end will come in five full cycles, for five, the difference between the Earth's number and that of the Gleaming Dawn Star, is the number of these children of warfare.

Sun symbol.

168

Gateway at Labna.

"As a sign to you that the end is nearing, My Father's Temple will be uncovered. Remember this in the days which are coming.

For a moment the Prophet stood quietly. When He began again His voice was softer, and once more it held unshed teardrops.

"Once there was a Man who dreamed of a New World, of one without war and sickness. He wished to see the people happy, and so He fought sacrifice and slavery. To this dream He gave of his life-blood. He knew that this was the desire of the Great Spirit, but suddenly there came upon him mocking visions.

"A horrible gift had come upon Him. He could look down the cycles of the Dawn Star and see into the distant future. It would have been well if what He was seeing was the redemption of suffering mankind, but this was not what He was seeing.

"Tula was bereft with a savage earthquake. Then came the Sacrificers. Blood dripped from the altars of idols. The same He saw in other cities.

169

Serpent Symbol, from pottery.

"The visions were even worse in Colula. The streets ran red with the blood of fighting. First, even upon our Temple, He saw the blood of Sacrificing. Then came even a more hideous carnage. There was fighting up the tiers of the Temple!"

The people drew in their breaths as one being, whispering in shocked tones to one another:

"What manner of men would commit such heresy?"

After a pause, the Prophet continued:

"Soul-sick from these hideous visions, the Man sought the comfort of a mountain, to be alone and near the God-head. He must renew His will for teaching, or pray for death that the visions be ended; for they told Him that His work was mockery in this future, if indeed there was a future.

"There in the silence and cold of the mountain a great sorrow was laid upon him, and the man sank down in the softness of the snowdrifts and prayed for either death or guidance.

"Then the heavens spoke in a crash of thunder, and the lightning flashed above the valley. The Man turned to look again on Tula, His most beloved city. Behold! It was naught but a mass of rubble.

"He wept there with great sorrow. He clung to the rocks, staring back toward Tula.

"Then the heavens growled with reverberations which shook the mountain like a rabbit. A flash of white light crashed beside Him and cracked across the night's darkness. Behold! The old heaven and earth were swept away, as if the cycle He had been seeing was smashed, and He looked into another.

"The heavens parted and a rising gold sun shone down on another Tula. Plainly He could see the valley, but the city was one He knew not. Magnificent was this Golden Tula!

"The Man was lifted beyond the cold earth. No longer He saw the Age of Destruction. Gone was the horrible Age of Warfare. He was looking beyond the Age of Carnage!"

The Prophet stopped and stared about Him. He looked on the eyes turned up to Him. He looked on the young and on the aged, on the masses who followed each word in silence. Then, softly, He continued:

"Walk with me through this Age of the Future. Tula shines in all of its glory, but the metals are of types we know not. Loving hands have rebuilt the parkways, have paved the streets, have rebuilt the temples. There is a great building where books are kept for the scholars, and many are those who come to read them. Tula is a great Center of Culture.

"Come with me to the New Colula. Shining again is My Father's Temple! Once more the city is filled with fountains and the parkways are wire-netted for the birds of rare plumage, and those who sing to enchant the listener. Cross through the Parkway to My Father's Temple. You will see again the same inscriptions which today your eyes are seeing, but now all people can read them.

"Come to the metropolis of the future. Here are buildings unlike those we fashion, yet they have a breathless beauty.

Feathered serpent symbol from antique pottery.

Here people dress in materials we know not, travel in manners beyond our knowledge, but more important than all this difference are the faces of. the people. Gone is the shadow of fear and suffering, for man no longer sacrifices, and he has outgrown the wars of his childhood. Now he walks full-statured toward his destiny - into the Golden Age of Learning.

"Carry this vision on through the ages, and remember Kate-Zahl, the Prophet."*

Serpent symbol, from pottery.

(*Sources: Song of Quetzal-Coatl, Sedillio and Bancroft, and Mayan legends.)

Kate-Zahl Preaches To The Mayans

FROM YUCATAN to Guatemala moved the figure of the Prophet. Through all the cities of the Mayans, along their wide, tree-shaded highways, from gleaming temple went Kate-Zahl's golden sandals. Escorted by the greatest nobles, thus touched by His reflected splendor, the Prophet was welcomed throughout the Broad Land.

Again various names were given the Pale God: Gu-ku-matz, the Plumed Serpent; or Kul-kul-kan, Lord of Wind and Water. Of the latter, kul is feather and kan is king-serpent.

To the Itzaes He was Itz-amna, the ancient hero of their migrations returned to them from over the Sunrise Ocean from whence He had led them in ancient times from the Red Land of their beginning. It is said that the Prophet, when He walked among them, founded one of their loveliest cities.

They say that His shrines are to be found in the ruins of Copan, Palenque, Kabah and Ux-mul, and though some were founded after His visit, His shrines still carried His sacred mementoes: his mantle, a pair of golden sandals, or rocks which had borne his weight for a moment. More precious than jewels are these to the Mayans.

To all these shrines ran the boulevards from the four directions marking upon the land the Great Cross, and upon them the people came with their products, their seeds, their animals and children to say their prayers and ask His blessing.

173

The Hand Kabul

And The Legend Of Itza-Mal

I N ITZA-MAL the people called Him Itza-Matul or the Silver Dew Which Falls From Heaven, because when He was asked of them His true name, answered:

"I come as the dew which falls from heaven."

Ever after they called Him Itza-Matul. After He left them a shrine was built which became one of the most famous in the Broad Land. This is how it happened.

On the morning when the Healer came to Itza-Mal and gave His strange name to the people, He mounted an old mound to lecture to them. During His warm impassioned phrases in which He spoke of things most holy and walked with them into the future, He pressed His hands down on an ancient altar, which was a large block of granite.

Many years after His departure, as the people came back to the ruin grieving, a miracle had happened.

There plainly so that everyone could see it, pressed down into the slab of the granite, was the imprint of the hands of the Prophet. The Hand Kabul, or the Hand Which Is Skillful, which everyone knew belonged to the Healer because of its strange marking, as if the Great Cross had been burned through it.

When the priesthood had been called to witness, they immediately erected a temple about the sacred slab of granite. A giant causeway running to the Four Directions was erected so that the people could come along the arms of the Great Cross to witness the Miracle of Itza-Mal and touch the rock which He had enchanted.

There are other shrines of the Hand Kabul, but they are never seen by White Man. Only from the airplane one can see the lifted highways which still mark the Great Cross,

Modern concept of The Prophet.

as the jungle has climbed up and across them; but the Hand Kabul has been carried from temple to temple, always deeper into the jungles. This relic which was left them by the Prophet and prized by the people beyond any jewels or goldwork, is always guarded and never, never left unattended.

The Scarab Ring

ONE OF THE most illuminating stories of the Prophet began with a scarab ring.

The lights were low and the conversation was interspersed with the tinkle of glasses at this rather boresome banquet when the woman who sat beside me held up her wine glass for a refilling. That is when I saw the scarab ring. It was like and yet unlike that of the Egyptian for it was cut in jade. I had never known jade to be used by the Egyptians. She was quick to notice my interest and took it off for me to see it better. Her words anticipated my question.

"No, it is not Egyptian. The ring is Mayan and it came from the Rain Well of the Ancients."

"Then it was worn by a bride of the Rain God before she was hurled to her death in the water?"

"Ah. I see you know my people."

"Your people? You most certainly are a Caucasian."

"Indeed I am, and so is my husband, but long ago we tired of this world and retired to another in the Mayan jungle."

"How did it happen?"

"We were flying our plane over the jungles. We were so fascinated with the lifted line of the highways and the living peaks which mark the pyramids, for they are also marked by the rise of the jungle. You know that there are hundreds of unknown ruins?"

"So I have been told. But how did you . . ."

"We ran out of gas."

"That is the hard way to begin an adventure."

"We did not exactly seek the Mayans. We were thrust upon them. It was years before we got out of the jungles, older and wiser than when we entered, for we saw things never seen by 'White Man', and indeed unguessed even by writers."

"Could you unbend to tell me a trifle?"

"Only if our name is never mentioned."

"It has already been forgotten."

"We came upon living Mayan cities, unknown and undreamed of by modern peoples. Here they live in the ancient splendor, but disguised so that the airplanes will not see them. They wish no contact with your world, and if they knew we had told, then they would kill us."

"Do they still have books, and can they read them?"

She turned and consulted her husband.

"We cannot answer that question."

"Very well. Tell me about the highways."

"The whole land is networked with them. Many of them are better than your best highways, if once they were to be freed from the jungle. They are built of cement much harder than you use which had been laid on a nine-foot flagging of sandstone. They are from sixty to a hundred feet wide."

"Why are the Mayans afraid to meet us, and why do they stay in hiding?"

"You have read of course of the Conquest?"

"But that was back in the Sixteenth Century."

"Have you ever heard of the Prophet? Of Hurukan or Zac-Mutul, the Mighty, which in Mayan means the Saintly One Who Worshipped No Idols?"

"Do you mean the Plumed Serpent?"

"I do indeed."

Her husband leaned across her.

"Have you heard of The Predictions?"

"You mean He foretold the coming of White Man?"

"Then you know what they know - that White Man's cycle is not yet over. He told them to wait and stay hidden."

"Yes, I know, but . . ."

"Before that He predicted the return of the Sacrificers?"

"An amazing foretelling of the rise of the Aztecs."

"Well, these people of ours are the White Priesthood," she answered. "They are the People who follow the Prophet. They fled before the rise of the Aztecs."

"Fantastic."

"Not as strange as the rites in their temples. We belong to them. They are the True Christians. We love them and we respect them."

Again she turned to her husband.

"You are not now going to stop talking? Turn not from the thirsty when you have water. I have followed this Legend across two continents."

"Very well, we will tell you a little. The High Priest whose title is Ah-Pope, is dressed like Quetzal-Coatl from the white mantle to the golden sandals. Did you know it was from our people that He accepted the wide waist wrap: a long cloth heavy with golden embroidery and encrusted with jewels, worn wrapped above the waistline? He accepted it as His badge of office, and carried it with Him across the ocean."

"Yes, I knew that in Yucatan He added it to His costume."

"I have seen the Hand Kabul, and about that I shall not comment. I have a strange veneration for the Prophet, and I do not wish to talk about Him. But I will tell you this: on top of the pyramids burns a sacred fire - not the one worshipped by the Sacrificers but the very fire first lighted by the Prophet."

"Tell me the religion of these pyramids."

"The Mayans are a friendly people, but they will not tell explorers or tourists about their pyramids. If you should ask them about the Thirteen Steps to the Fire, they will say that each is some god which they have forgotten, but behind their hands, the people are smiling. Only if like us, you live among them, and then join their worship, will you learn what the pyramid stands for.

"The Sacred Fire which was lighted almost two thousand years ago is tended by the Ah-Pope or the reigning Kate-Zahl and his twelve disciples. They have been chosen from the time of the Prophet by the 'laying on of hands' one to the other, and each is chosen for his great soul-stature. It takes real soul-stature to reach the Fire.

"The Ah-Pope hears confessions if the people wish to give them, and advises his flock in all their ways of living. He presides at weddings, baptismals and burials. He blesses the animals in the springtime and the seeds for planting. In

Macoba.

the fall he blesses the crops for the Thanksgiving ceremony.

"Those who do not get close to the people never learn the meaning of the pyramid, as I said. It is a religion of daily living, not words to be mouthed on Sunday and forgotten on Monday. Every step upward is an honor to be earned. Yet it is also possible to step down, and is much more easily done than to go up.

"The lowest step is the fundamental Step of the entire religion, as taught by the Prophet.

1) Commit no petty act. As you would be treated so treat your fellows. You cannot follow this religion and the law of the jungle. If in your life you follow the law of the jungle, then walk away.

"The other steps are as follows:

2) Seek the spirit of truth. Never accept half-truths. Upon this foundation build your life and thought, your work and worship.

3) Of the work of your existence, do your own share. No man or woman can hope to enter blessedness borne upon the backs of servants.

Chichanchob, Casa Colorado, Red House.

"Those are the fundamentals.

"The next seven steps of the pyramid are the Ten Commandments in identical order except that they are condensed.

"The last three steps are not only secret, but they demand a soul so saintly that none but the finest may ever surmount them. As the Plumed Serpent said:

" 'Many hear the call but few are chosen.'

"One of the greatest tasks of the Plumed Serpent is to conduct the chants. The work of this he may divide up among his priesthood. One of those chants was spoken by the people when the Healer was leaving the country. It is hauntingly like one I learned at my mother's knee in childhood.

"On Thanksgiving we chant this before the pyramid:

" 'We bring to thee, oh Father, divine spirit who has no image, this fruit of our yearly labor, as of old thine own son taught us. Bless these seeds, oh most holy, that we may make the earth more fruitful. Bless this corn, oh most powerful, and help us live up to thy instructions.' "

180

Her husband leaned toward me again.

"My wife may be talking too much. She gets carried away. Let me say this. The pyramid symbolizes the spiritual life of the soul. This religion leaves no loopholes for double-dealing or cheating to hide, be forgiven and continue a dozen times. Insincerity breaks the fundamental First Law. This is a living religion and one is daily reminded of the holy man who came here with His wealth of geographical knowledge, and His ability to speak perhaps a thousand languages, yet His warm humanity, His great love and fineness of soul are reflected in these His People, so that He lives for you even in the Twentieth Century. It is something like a miracle. Yes, our little heaven is a sort of lost Shangri-la, and we shall never disclose its location."

There was a kind of finality in his voice, so I addressed my next question to her.

"Just one more question: could you tell me something of His departure?"

She hesitated a moment and then with a few brief sentences painted the picture of that sad day of parting, while I marvelled that such a vivid scene could come down through the centuries with all the freshness of a yesterday. He nudged her arm and she stopped, smiling at me apologetically. However, I noticed that she pulled out a sheet of scratch paper, which later turned out to be a bill, and scribbled something on the back. This she pressed into my hand as we left, and to keep him from knowing, if it was important, I said laughingly:

"Just think what I might have missed if it had not been for a scarab ring."

YUCATAN

An Amerind Of The Mayans
Views A Scientific Problem

THE FASCINATING work done in Yucatan near Merida and published in the January, 1959 National Geographic Magazine came to the attention of the author. As to most students of the cultures of the Americas, this expedition with its excavations spread much light in dark places. According to Mayan dates, which we are able to decipher because of their inter-revolving astronomical calendars, the Mayans built most of their Yucatan cities during the sixth and seventh century A.D. Yet their legends are much older. Was it possible that the Mayans came north from Guatemala, and this was the locale of the earlier legends? This is the contradiction which faced scholars up to the excavations undertaken jointly by the National Geographic Society and Tulane University at Dzibilchaltun, which means "where there is writing on the rocks".

Here the scientists had found a surprise. Dr. E. Wyllys Andrews, the expedition leader, found an entire sequence in pottery design which for the first time gave science a sort of timetable. Pottery, artifacts and architecture here indicate that this city was founded between 2000 and 1000 B.C. if not earlier. It continued to function throughout Mayan history as a great metropolis right up to the time of the Spanish Conquest.

The culture developed on the spot and flowered through the Classic Period when the city was perhaps the largest in the Americas. Instead of being abandoned with the decline of the Classic Period, as is the usual case, the city continued throughout all the turning points of Mayan history.

The descriptions of the site are most intriguing. The city was the largest thus discovered by any excavators. It is

Sabachtsche.

estimated that it was about one third as large as modern
Mexico City. According to the statistics given me in that
metropolis during 1955, the ancient city of the Mayans
then should have a population of about two million souls.

The great ceremonial highway through the city running
from palace to temple is sixty feet wide and some twenty
miles in length. Of course it will be many years before the
herculean task of excavation has been completed and more
information is available to science.

One fact greatly puzzled the excavators. They found a
temple probably dating from the Classic Period to the time
of the Spanish Conquest. It had been credited to about 500
A.D. by carbon dating and was finally destroyed by what
were probably the weapons of the Spanish. During this last
gasp of the temple as a Mayan institution, the Indians
themselves turned archaeologist. They tunneled down through
their floor to another older temple, perhaps entering a
secret passage left open to the ancient shrine. Here they
cleaned away the rubble and rededicated it. Now they
fashioned a plaster tube leading into the rubble below. At

183

the bottom of the shaft they placed seven small clay figures. No scientist had never seen anything like them. Each exhibited some deformity. Two were hunchbacks, one a dwarf and another had a swollen stomach. The excavators could only guess at the significance. There were educated guesses that this was some sort of healing rite.

The Mayans then erected an altar just two steps away from the opening of the tube. Embedded in the center was a T-shaped symbol with a striking medallion in the middle. Nearby stood tall, brilliantly colored incense burners, sculptured in clay in the stylized image of the brutal sanguinary gods of what the Prophet called the Sacrificers, but the scientists call "the Aztec influence of Mayan decadence". The medallion itself, covered with calendric and divinatory hieroglyphs, is apparently the key object.

Fascinated with this interesting problem of the present, the author sought out a family of Mayan friends. They listened with interest touched with what seemed to be a shade of amusement. When I finished, they began speaking to one another in Mayan which closed me out of the conversation, for I understand very little of the ancient American language. However, I did catch the name "Kul-kul-kan" repeated several times. Finally unable to stand the suspense any longer, I broke in.

"Are you by any chance speaking of the Lord of Wind and Water?"

"Yes, we were. I understand that you are interested in the Fair God, and therefore you should know that He was kindly disposed to all misformed people such as dwarfs and hunchbacks. He always healed them. Furthermore, He also took a kindly interest in pregnant women, whom He never failed to stop and bless."

"I realize that, and also the significance of the T-symbol and the calendar medallion; but this took place during the reign of the Sacrificers, apparently shortly before the Spanish destroyed the temple!"

"Very well. Let me tell a story and you will understand."

He glanced at his Mayan friends and family and cleared his throat.

"For centuries the people had watched the calendar pass around from circle to circle. From each inner circle to the next outer circle it went. As predicted, the Sacrificers came back; even as He had caused it to be inscribed. Always it drew nearer to the Time of Warning. As that date approached, the Emperor Moctezoma decreed that it be taken down and buried. He changed the calendar. Thus he reasoned that he had erased the fateful prediction of long retribution against the Sacrificers. In whispers the people still remembered. The bloody sacrificing was continuing in all the temples, even in His temple in Colula.

"Then came the year when He had told them to expect the Bearded Pale Ones clothed in metal garments, carrying rods which made a loud noise and killed at a distance. The people were frightened. They had not forgotten.

"Finally a day came during the Year of Retribution, when the Bearded Ones were sighted. And of all days, it came on the Feast Day Sacred to the Prophet! Flashing across the Broad Land with obsidian mirrors came the fateful message: 'The Bearded Pale Ones are landing. They are dressed in metal and carry rods which kill at a distance.'

"Here in this Mayan city the Sacrificing Priesthood decided to try to reverse destiny. They remembered a long-neglected religion, and an almost forgotten altar. They tunneled down to His altar in mad haste. It had been covered in burial long centuries before. They made figurines which might catch His attention. They burned candles of His incense in the only candle-holders or incense holders they had. They prayed night and day, but we know that their efforts were for naught. The Spanish marched in and took the city now deserted by the panic-stricken people. Who would defend it? No one but a fool. This is the true story of the Mayan temple."

Cosmul Island

THERE IS a shrine in Yucatan more sacred than any other; more beloved than that of Hunab-Ku, the God Who Has No Image, more dear to the hearts of the people than the magnificent ruins of their cities such as the Temple of the Thousand Columns. That shrine is an island whose very soil is sacred, for it was from here that the Prophet left in the Serpent vessel for the Land of Tla-Pallan.

Cosmul is a jungle island, once a part of the land behind it and a part of the eastern seacoast which is in the process of slowly sinking. In the time-clock of geology such a subsidence is not an over-night event. To suggest that it happened less than seventeen or eighteen hundred years ago would invite scientific skepticism, for Cosmul is now twelve miles from the shoreline. Yet there is a great highway with its lifted line of trees streaking across the jungle to Cosmul, a roadway which, with its huge nine-foot sandstone flagging and hard cement cover, dips down under the waves at the coast-line and again reappears on the dry land of the ancient seaport.

The docks of the busy merchant vessels have long since rotted away, and the ships which tied up here have vanished; but in legends, Cosmul comes to life.

Especially vivid are the tales of the coming of the beautiful Serpent vessel, and how the grieving people waited day and night near it in order to have a place of vantage when the milling thousands would come pouring down the highway in a human tide to watch the Prophet board His ship, on that day which was different, and never to be forgotten.

The Serpent Vessel

FROM OUT of the sunrise, one warm spring morning, toward the Itzae Country and the island named Cosmul, the people gathered to watch a strangely beautiful ocean vessel approaching. Of deepest redwood it was fashioned, very shining and highly polished. Its sides were carved inter-twining serpents of black and red.

The bow was fashioned high and curling, ending with the head of a monstrous dragon, while the stern sloped up to a tail. Upon the highest part of the back deck was a golden throne draped with cloths of beauty, and about the throne sat richly garbed strangers.

Along the lower deck were many oarsmen, and the rhythmical lifting of their paddles made the ship strangely resemble a centipede-legged monster crawling rapidly over the water toward them. This was not new to the people. Often trading vessels had many oarsmen.

Now the people whispered together:

"This is the ship which has come for the Prophet. He said that a ship would come to Cosmul to take Him far away to Tla-Pallan, the beautiful island across the ocean where wonderful news is waiting for Him."

"Yea. This must indeed be the vessel. It is not from any well-known nation. They bring no goods; only the strangers."

"Then I, for one, shall remain by the vessel, so that when the dawn of the Departure comes, I shall be able to see Him leaving."

And the man sat down upon his blanket.

All day people came to see the vessel; and as the days passed by, more people remained there, eating and sleeping beside the strange ship like a swarm of little lost children - waiting.

The Departure

FOUR DAYS passed, and the crowds who were waiting watched the sunlight reflect on the vessel from the gently heaving water, coating with gold the shining serpents; or the moon, cool-shining, painting the vessel with brushes of silver. Still they had not seen the Healer. Then came a morning that was different.

From far away arose a strange new sighing, borne on the wind from afar off, like the torrent of a distant river. The people who had been waiting looked into each other's eyes and nodded.

"This is the day of His departure."

Closer came the lamentations, like the surge of a flood onrushing, and a wave of people engulfed the highway. The cries came from the throats of untold thousands, jostling each other for a place of vantage. Yet the greatest noise was still in the distance; louder and stronger it kept approaching, greater than any sounds of the jungle, more mighty than the wildest windstorm, deep-throated like advancing rapids.

Onward came the human torrent, and above it the plaintive sighing like the churning of a river as it fell downward over a steep cliff into the splash of a million raindrops.

Now the priesthood was making a pathway, trying to hold back the people. Through this path came the conch-shell marchers followed by the deep-sounding tom-toms, then the tall and powerful oarsmen, who walked up to the vessel and drew up stiffly there beside it.

San Miguel, Island of Cosmul.

Next came the great men of all the Nations. Led by the Monarch of the Toltecs, resplendent in his magnificent costume, and his vast assemblage of courtiers, came the Chichimecs, the Itzaes, Azpotecs and many others. Some were distant unheard-of nations in strange and colorful costumes, garbed in every shade of the rainbow, some flashing with embroidery and jewels, some clothed partly with leather and trimmed in other fashions. All the faces showed deep sorrow, and their crowns of magnificent plumage were bowed. This morning the people had no eyes for splendor.

Now came the bearded strangers, with their strangely fashioned mantles, and only they smiled as they passed, bowing. Behind them were more of the white-robed priesthood, wafting incense and chanting softly. Some among them were openly weeping.

Far back on the highway now came the crying, and one could tell by the lamentations just where the Prophet was passing. To the men near the vessel that sound grew steadily stronger, until, held high above the people so that all could see Him without pushing, came the litter carrying the Feathered Serpent.

Clothed in a white robe of spotless seed-silk, with the

189

Tuloom.

wide golden scarf of the Mayan High Priest wrapped about
Him above the waist-line, His face was sad as He looked
down on the people. In an unending series of blessings, the
silent figure of the Pale God passed.

By the time His platform had reached the vessel, the
strangers had climbed to their places, and the rowers had
seated themselves at their benches. Now the Prophet stepped
from His platform and mounted to the ship's high deck where
the Golden Seat of Honor awaited Him.

There He turned and faced the people. Now, at last,
everyone could see Him, and the crush of pushing was
ended.

Never before or since, in all the Broad Land was ever
heard such a terrible silence. Never since has it been known
in the jungle. Hungrily the people sought His features, at
once so peaceful and so lofty, sought the beauty of His white
halo shining in the morning sunlight like a mist of gold about
Him. Sadly they fastened their eyes upon him, knowing this
was goodbye forever; trying to remember each tiny detail so
they could tell their children's children, to be passed onward
through the ages.

190

Others held aloft their babies saying:

"Look once more upon Him. Glory is He of all the nations! Look upon Him and remember."

One man was heard to cry out, as if the words were torn from him:

"Mightiest Prophet of all the ages! His face, so noble, is like a mighty, echoing fire-flame, which for us must be extinguished!"

Now He held up His hand for silence, the sacred Hand Kabul, and He turned and looked upon all the faces. On babes held aloft to see Him, upon the old and on the youthful, those eyes so grey-green, like the deep sea, rested fleetingly and passed on as the flowing of water, but each rest was a benediction, and each one felt that instant of blessing.

Someone began chanting an olden chant which He had taught them, but since has become known as the Chant of Cosmul.

"Almighty Father who created all mankind, and bound us here in this realm of service, open to us thy hand of mercy, that we may have shelter and food for our bodies.

"Oh, you who dwell in the golden sunshine, in the liquid silver which falls from the rain clouds, in the depths of the sea and the power of the wind storm, Our Father, who art in heaven, most holy is thy word.

"Guide us, oh Father, through life's trail of hardships, deliver us from all that is evil, for thine is the power from the ice to the lava, and thine is the glory forever and ever."

The Prophet held up His hand again in final benediction, then turning in majestic silence, seated himself, His white robes falling about His sandals and whirling away in a torrent of black crosses.

At this signal the ropes which held the vessel were loosened and the ship began to turn out to sea.

Then the Prophet again stood and faced back toward the people, holding up His hand in benediction and farewell.

The cries of the people broke forth like terrible thunder as the Prophet once more seated himself and the ship rapidly moved toward the skyline. The crying must have echoed woefully after Him as His ship shrank in proportions, for it continued long after the ship had gone. Yet as long as the vessel could be seen, every eye followed it and the dot of white on the Golden Seat of Honor, until at last it vanished along with the ship that held it and wavered into the teardrops which blended that distant-stretching horizon.

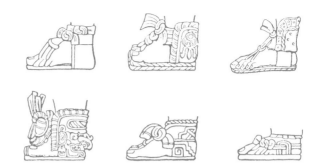

Epilogue

The Prophet's sandals.

No one ever again saw the Serpent vessel. No one ever returned to tell the people whether He reached Tla-Pallan. And though, through the Dawn Star's returning cycles, that double star of morn and evening sometimes called the Star of Our Master, Tlau-izcal-pan-ticutli, much has happened on the dates He predicted, yet never again in all the Broad Land, among the many waiting nations, has been heard the tread of those golden sandals, nor seen the beloved face of Kate-Zahl, the Prophet.

Front of the Casa de Las Tortugas at Uxmal.

Finis

O ENDS THE Tale of Times Long Vanished; of cities which live now but in story; of Puants, Itzaes and wealthy Toltecs as well as other exotic empires not listed among the living nations.

So ends the drama of Mahnt-Azoma, sometimes called Kate-Zahl the Prophet, Mighty Plumed Water Serpent, whose words are repeated at council fires whenever the ancient ones are gathered. The back-drop is not the land as we know it, for the climates are much changed. The mines are under a forest blanket; the Valley of the Gardens is now a desert; the highways are covered by a strangling jungle; while the city described by a hundred nations is now but a long lost legend. Yet strung together, they form a pattern which becomes a string of pearls, long scattered. The chanters may live far away from each other, but the mystic figure never changes. The phrases falling from the lips of wild non-Christians like the Seri are hauntingly familiar; the marked palms are miraculous in healing, while the sea-eyes are dark with untold sorrow as they look through the Cycles of the Future.

So ends the Legend of the Pale God, yet that end is shrouded with questions. Who were the strangers of the Serpent vessel? Where is the Land of Tla-Pallan? What was the news which He was seeking? And most intriguing of all: who was this lonely wandering figure? No man can answer that recurring question and place a period after his answer; for it will return again like a spectre.

Such is the legend of the Prophet.

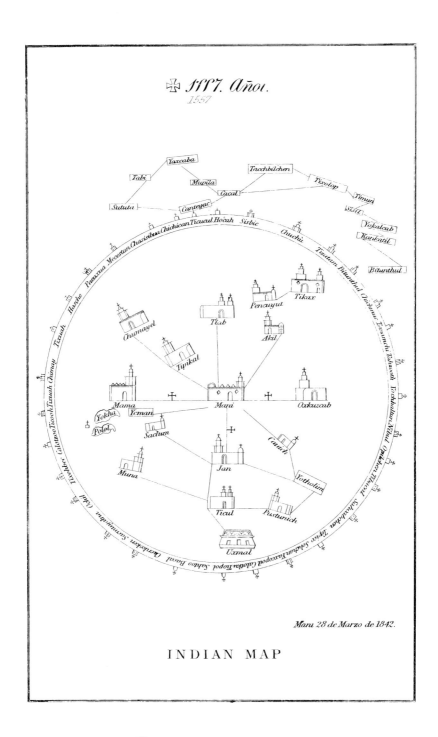

✠ 𝓢𝓢𝓢𝓥. 𝓐ñ𝓸ι.
1557

Yaxcaba
Tabi
Mupila
Tacchbilchen
Cacal
Tixotop
Timun
Sututa
Canteyac
Sisil
Yokalcab
Kankatil
Pacaxua Mecostan Chassivbun Chichican Ticual Hocah Sisbic
Ouchu
Tixatan Brianthid
Bibunthid
Hoxte
Tixuah
Chichuac Taxanchi Tahaxoth
Chumayel
Pencuyut
Tikax
Tixah Chamay
Tiab
Akil
Tipikal
Tixooh
Tixxah
Colatxoo
Tixebxee
Morhhatlian Xibxd
Opchen Tixoxl
Mama
Yeman
Mani
Oxkuzcab
Yokha
Sacbithan
Aliborob Ixxxd
Polol
Sactun
Canah
Muna
Yotholin
Jan
Ticul
Pustunich
Uxmal

Manı 28 de Marzo de 1842.

INDIAN MAP

195

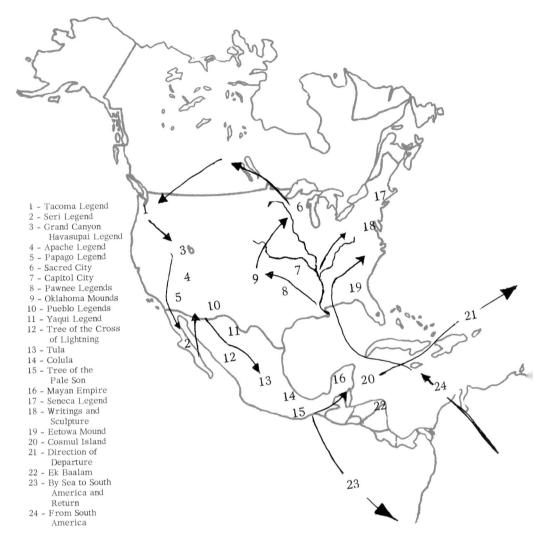

1 - Tacoma Legend
2 - Seri Legend
3 - Grand Canyon
    Havasupai Legend
4 - Apache Legend
5 - Papago Legend
6 - Sacred City
7 - Capitol City
8 - Pawnee Legends
9 - Oklahoma Mounds
10 - Pueblo Legends
11 - Yaqui Legend
12 - Tree of the Cross
    of Lightning
13 - Tula
14 - Colula
15 - Tree of the
    Pale Son
16 - Mayan Empire
17 - Seneca Legend
18 - Writings and
    Sculpture
19 - Eetowa Mound
20 - Cosmul Island
21 - Direction of
    Departure
22 - Ek Baalam
23 - By Sea to South
    America and
    Return
24 - From South
    America

The Prophet moved from South America up the Mississippi and by rivers throughout the Eastern states. From Michigan he went to Canada and from there to the Pacific Coast. Moving from there to the Pacific tribes by way of Grand Canyon and Havasupai, he went to the Pueblos and then down the Chichihua Valley to Tula and later Cholula. He apparently sailed with the merchants to South America. Returning, he left for the Mayan Empire and finally departed from Cosmul Island by ship for an island lying toward the sunrise over the sea.

196

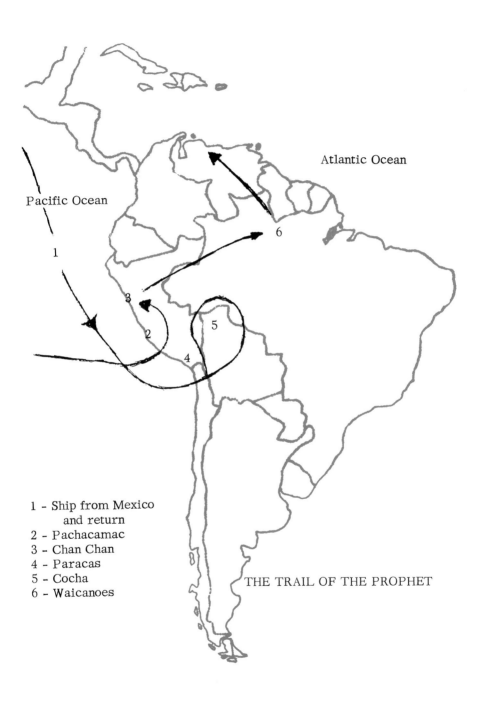

Pacific Ocean

Atlantic Ocean

1 - Ship from Mexico
     and return
2 - Pachacamac
3 - Chan Chan
4 - Paracas
5 - Cocha
6 - Waicanoes

THE TRAIL OF THE PROPHET

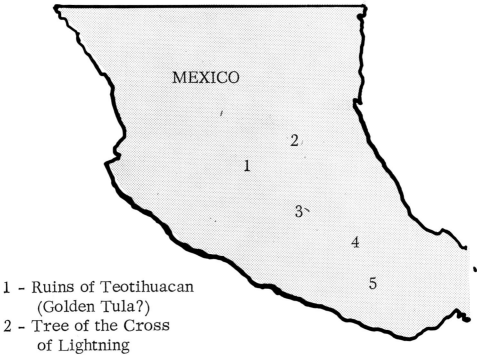

MEXICO

2

1

3

4

5

PACIFIC OCEAN

1 - Ruins of Teotihuacan
    (Golden Tula?)
2 - Tree of the Cross
    of Lightning
3 - Ancient Colula
4 - Ancient Giant Tree
5 - Ruins of Mitla and
    Monte Alban
6 - Numerous Unexplored
    Ruins
7 - Ruins of Palenque
8 - Numerous Ruins
9 - Mayan New Empire
    (roughly 500 AD to
    Conquest)

10 - Ruins of Uxmal
11 - City and Highway of
     Dzibil-Chaltun now
     being excavated
     (over 3000 years old)
12 - Ruins of Chichen Itza
13 - The Prophet's Place
     of Departure
14 - Numerous Unexplored
     Ruins
15 - Ruins of Copan
16 - Legend of the Tiger
17 - Ek Baalam
18 - Mayan Old Empire
     (roughly before 500 AD)

GULF OF MEXICO

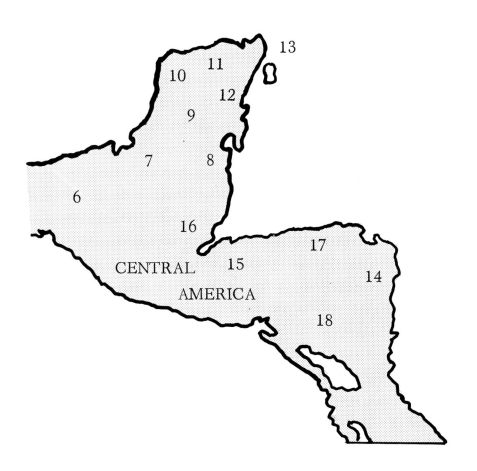

CENTRAL

AMERICA

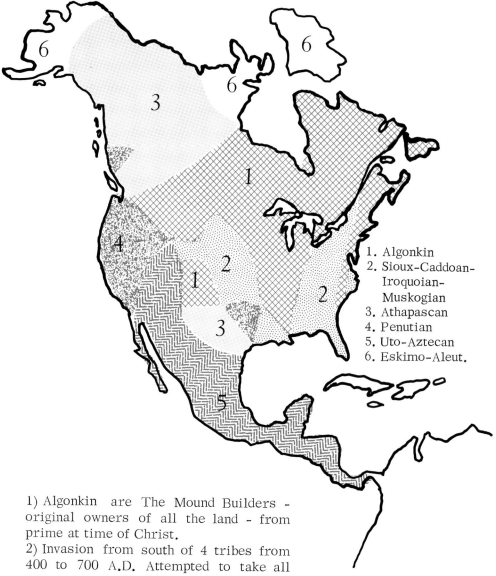

1. Algonkin
2. Sioux-Caddoan-
   Iroquoian-
   Muskogian
3. Athapascan
4. Penutian
5. Uto-Aztecan
6. Eskimo-Aleut.

1) Algonkin are The Mound Builders - original owners of all the land - from prime at time of Christ.

2) Invasion from south of 4 tribes from 400 to 700 A.D. Attempted to take all country west - leaving some fragments.

3) Asian Invasion - one fragment reaching Ariz.-New Mexico 700-1000 A.D.

4) Penutian - very old - language separation greater than Arabic and English 22 nations.

5) Uto-Aztecan - after fall of Toltecs small groups pushed north and were absorbed by various peoples - one group are Pueblos - 500-700 A.D.

6) Eskimo-Aleut. as yet not well understood.

200

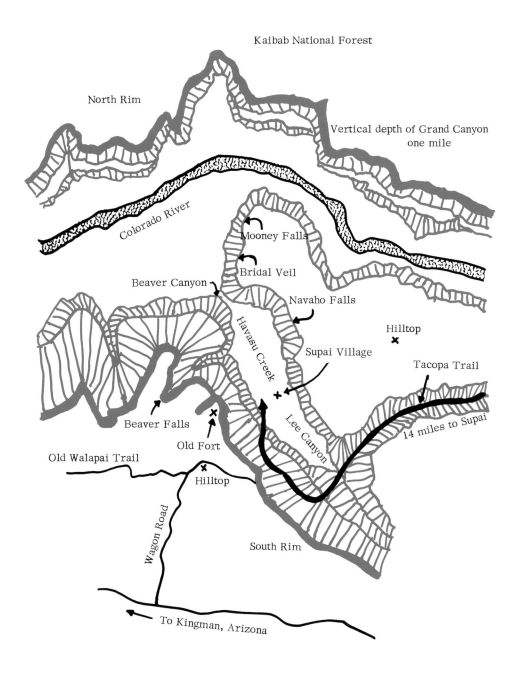

LOCATION OF LEGENDARY TACOPA TRAIL
TO HAVASUPAI INDIAN VILLAGE, ARIZONA

Kaibab National Forest

North Rim

Vertical depth of Grand Canyon
one mile

Colorado River

Mooney Falls

Bridal Veil

Beaver Canyon

Navaho Falls

Hilltop

Supai Village

Tacopa Trail

Havasu Creek

14 miles to Supai

Beaver Falls

Old Fort

Lee Canyon

Old Walapai Trail

Hilltop

Wagon Road

South Rim

To Kingman, Arizona

201

The Identity Of The Prophet

THE IDENTITY OF the Plumed Serpent, or the Lord-of-Wind-and-Water was an argument which raged with considerable heat at the time of the Conquest. The Catholic Church, confronted with the facts which seemed to point to an early Christian, suggested that He may have been St. Thomas. In fact, in Mexico, He was often called St. Quetzal-Coatl.

La Casas and Kingsborough were not inclined to accept this conclusion. They pointed out that such words as sin, Trinity, Virgin-birth, winged-beings or angels, the use of the ten commandments, and the ceremonial baptism and marriage vows whose similarity extends across both American continents suggests an origin for which Lord Kingsborough was inclined to look higher than St. Thomas, while the monk remained discreetly silent.

It is the opinion of the present writer that Kate-zahl must have been an Essene. Since the opening of the Dead Sea Scrolls, we have come to know a good deal about this religious order of which Jesus was supposed to have been a member. We know now that they favored a white toga-like garment, wore no covering on their heads, and always spoke of God as "My Father".

Strangely enough, the Amerind, or American Indian, seems to recognize this word. I have been corrected several times in its pronounciation. Finally a Choctah informed me that this was the name for the Wind God. Although the name may differ from tribe to tribe, he said it could be recognized by the long e sound repeated twice with a hissing in between. Therefore, this word should be Eessee-Nee. A few days later I brought him a temple painting of Osiris from Ancient

Egypt, and asked him if he could recognize the deity in question. Without any hesitation he named Osiris as the Wind God, and then as an added surprise, he pointed to Set and said: "That is the Death God."

When I argued that in this case the name was Osiris, he shook his head.

"These people are not dealing accurately with you. The ceremonial name should be E-see-rees."

"Yet in Mexico the Prophet was known as Quetzal or Kate-Zahl."

"That is the name of a bird which stood for the Wind or Air. Our name for Him was Ee-see-co-tl. The Tl sound is a title of great veneration."

Thus does one learn the most amazing facts from the Amerind, but the suggestion of ancient knowledge is even greater.

That Kate-Zahl made His amazing travels during the First Century would be far harder to disclaim today than it was during the lifetime of Alex Hrdlicka, the anthropologist who devoted his life to proving that the Amerind is a recent invader from the Orient. He so influenced the present writer when a student at the University of California, Southern Branch, that it was some time before I could take this legend seriously. Alas for Hrdlicka and his ideas, the discovery of flints of Amerind manufacture in the fossilized bones of bison undoubtedly Pleistocene or Ice-Age time was followed by the newest tool of science - carbon-dating. Then all the civilizations which Hrdlicka had pronounced very recent began to recede backward in time. Immediately the legend, which had been passed over, again sprang to life.

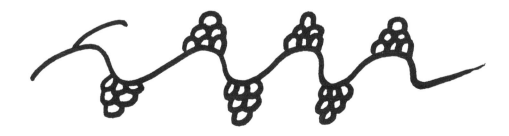

Cloud Serpent design.

I could no longer regard the figure of Kate-Zahl as a simple Dawn God who was opposed to the God of Darkness, that Aztec divinity Tezcat-li-poca. Especially was this true after I had met Sedillio. That sage was not unacquainted with the ideas of Hrdlicka, whom he regarded with amused indifference. Although grateful for the recitation of Sedillio's ancient chants, which, lacking sons and headed for battle, he might have taken to the grave, yet I was frankly skeptical of the antiquity of the Chihuahua Valley. Not until I had questioned pilots about the ancient drainage systems, and had flown over it myself, did I suddenly realize the authenticity of this legacy.

That Tezcat-li-poca was the final great leader of the Sacrificers as they marched to power now seems to me very probable. Perhaps he followed the Prophet in time, but he must have had a very powerful personality to overcome the veneration of the people for the Pale God.

By rereading old college notes taken so carelessly at the time which now have taken on new meaning; reading old books now lost but which are quoted by other old books; seeking out the stories told to the explorers by the tribes who then spoke freely because they were not silenced by later cynical amusement caused by ignorance; and especially by visiting the wild tribes, who, as Delugic, Chief Medicine Man of the Mescallero Apaches once said to me: are "willing to sit down and reason with you if you can contribute to the Council", has this book grown, but the identity of the Prophet who apparently did live in the First Century, still remains an illusive mystery.

Dr. Buck, late Curator of the Bishop Museum of Hawaii,

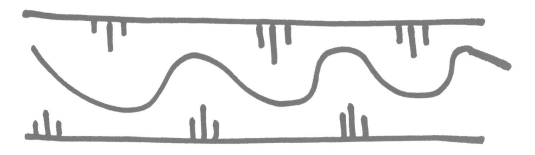

Variation of Cloud Serpent design.

was not surprised that Wako or Wakea was to be traced around the Americas. Numerous plants found in both areas had convinced him of ancient commerce, while his people who had travelled to all Pacific points by star-navigation regarded no distance across the Pacific as impossible. Therefore I am again thrown back upon Dr. Buck's description of the Fair God as a man who arrived in the company of men who apparently wore clothing Mediterranean in type, in three Roman ships, or again, in ships of a Mediterranean type, whose origin was probably the Red Sea.

However, Dr. Buck noted that China had similar legends and also India, which he had collected from natives of those lands then living in Hawaii. There is a Wako-yama mountain in Japan - the last word being Japanese for mountain. Therefore, he concluded that the ships which brought and left the Fair God had already toured the Orient, undoubtedly in His company.

Beyond the fact that he regarded Wako or Wakea as a real person who lived during the Century of Jesus, he was unwilling even to hazard a guess as to the identity of the Prophet.

Perhaps we should leave the question with the Mexican archaeologists, who when tossed this puzzle of antiquity, simply shrug their shoulders and answer:

According to the Dead Sea Scrolls there was a very saintly man preceding Jesus by about a century. This holy man, an Essene, had no name except "The Master" or "The Great Teacher". He was crucified but was apparently saved by the Essenes who were in the crowd surrounding Him. Scientists in England have suggested the Polynesian chants allow for an error of time - perhaps a century, plus or minus.

"Quien sabe? Who knows?"

Another variation of Cloud Serpent design.

The Hand Symbol

THE NORTH AMERICAN Indians used the figure of the human hand in their system of picture writing to denote supplication to the Great Spirit, a symbol of strength mastery and power. In all their great number of ceremonial practices and observances there is not a single one in which the symbol of the hand does not appear. The priests are drawn with hand outstretched or uplifted. At times it was one hand and arm, sometimes the other, but the most common was both. Among the northern tribes it is not a rare thing to see these hands drawn or depicted on bark, skins or even pieces of wood; intended by those who profess the arts of magic and prophecy, to aid and keep in memory the sacred songs and dances. Those on wood are more often found in the region of Lake Superior and the upper Mississippi, and are called "music boards".

One of these boards was obtained from a great meta or priest, many years ago, and was brought to a city and passed thru a rolling press. It was found to be covered with small figures on both sides of the board. There were forty principal figures on one side and six of them were of the uplifted hand, four of which were attached to an arm, the others of the hand alone. The reverse side carried thirty-eight characters, nine of which were the hand and one of these was connected with a torso. The import, as the meta said, was of musical symbolism.

The drawing of the hand is almost uniformly the same in all tribes of North America whether it be alone or joined to a body. In some cases it is easy to figure out its connection to music and dances or heroic ceremonies, but in others the use remains a mystery, but is regarded, by those

206

who have investigated, as a devotional sign of great importance to the Indians. Those who have lived among the tribes to learn of their costumes have found many instances of the "hand" alone as a symbol. Great secrecy is used in the lodges of the medicine men when preparations are being made for the decoration of those who are to take part in the sacred festive dances. The priests apply the marks upon the breast, shoulder or any part of the body by first smearing their hands with colored clay, and pressing them tight against the exposed body of the participant. Thus is conveyed the idea that a charm or mystic protection has been placed about the dancer and denotes his proficiency in the hidden arts. The use of the symbolic hand is found, not in a single tribe, but in all the tribes, Dacotahs, Winnebagoes and all others of the red race located in North America, most of whom speak a dialect derived from the language of the Algonquins.

There is a description of a village temple, which has been left by a man who visited there in 1831, and its location at that time was between Twelve Apostles' Island in Lake Superior and the Falls of St. Anthony, in the Chippewa country. It was a curious edifice on the edge of a dense forest. It was erected of stout posts set in circular form and was arranged in the manner of a sea shell causing the entrant to involve himself in a labyrinth. There was but one door and this was entered by the priests only, who were the head or political chiefs of the tribe. They were usually men of higher intellect than the rest and in this way perhaps they could hold an awed influence over their subjects, but the man who related this story had been allowed to go within this building and found there all the paraphenalia of the magic art of priesthood, and carved upon the naked wood of the walls were many hands and inscriptions. It was explained to him that these were symbols of importance and they were always to be found in the ancient hieroglyphics of their race.

The red hands which appeared in the far off land of Yucatan in the travels of John L. Stephens most likely connect the North American Indian tribes in some cabalistic way to those of Central America.

Notes

(Pronounced Wah-kay-ah)

Dr. Buck (now deceased) of Bishop Museum, Honolulu, and author of "Vikings of The Sunrise" in his letter upon Wakea, indicated that the white god of Polynesia was evidently a human being coming in three Roman-type ships from the direction of the Red Sea and could definitely be assigned to the Century of Christ, plus or minus some fifty years. He also spoke of similar legends throughout Asia reinforcing the date and manner of coming as well as origin, although not forsaken by the ships as He apparently was in Polynesia. Dr. Buck furthermore indicated that Wakea had evidently heard of the Polynesian skill at navigation and therefore decided to make use of it to make a further journey. Dr. Buck was much interested in hearing of the American Indian legends. He made no suggestions as to who Wakea may have been. Japan for example, has her Wako-yama. In Japanese, "yama" is the word for mountain. There is a mountain bearing that name where a white god is supposed to have taught. The legend recounted here is the one told the author by Dr. Buck, himself a full-blooded Polynesian.

SYMBOL OF THE DAWN STAR

The Phoenician symbol for the Hesperides or "Blessed Isles of the Atlantic" was Venus, or The Dawn Star. In those days the locations of certain lands were jealously guarded trade secrets. Dr. Swennhagen claims that Phoenician and Summerian inscriptions were to be viewed in certain sub-terranean Brazilian galleries while Braghine states that on a cliff behind Rio De Janeiro some miles in Havea are letters several feet in height which are inscribed upon the sheer cliff-face in cuneiform, undoubtedly carved by means of rope ladders hung from above. The inscription reads "Badezir of The Phoenician Tyre. The First son of Jethbaal".

Jethbaal ruled Tyre from 887 to 856 BC. This would furnish documentary proof of Phoenician trade if the above account is correct. The author has never been to this location, but would appreciate copies from natives of the region if possible. Cuneiform is a wedge-shaped script.

Since the priceless library of Ashburniphal, King of Babylon and first archaeologist, had been found and translated from the dead Sumerian into Babylonian with the aid of Ashburniphal's own dictionaries, archaeologists are going to have to revise the sources of such western learning as the "Phoenician alphabet", "Greek geometry", "Babylonian learning" and "Arabian astronomy". These were first Sumerian - a non-Semitic people of mysterious origin who preceded both the Semites and Aryan-speaking peoples into the Mediterranean. See Chiera's "They Wrote On Clay". The Sumerians handed the recognition of Venus as a star of importance down to Babylon from whence it became "The Star of David" to the Jews.

There is very good reason for the recognition of Venus as a symbol for the Americas from her Antillian islands to the ends of her lands. Venus is a highly-involved calendrical system in all of the more civilized nations, but the symbol and numbers are held sacred by all the wild tribes showing degeneration from ancient knowledge.

The Venus symbol is often connected with the Prophet, and no North American Indian tribe will make war or go into battle while Venus is shining.

MAORI ABILITY TO NAVIGATE

Skeptics are urged to read Dr. Frank Buck's "Vikings of The Sunrise".

THE JUNGLE

The Waikanoes are today one of the wildest of jungle tribes utterly untouched by any missionary influence. Their blow-guns with poison darts keep white men at a respectful distance.

209

THE CITY OF BALAAM

According to Quiche legend, this city of the Black Tiger was in existence since before the Deluge. See Bancroft. Legend recounted is one told by the wild Quiches of today, about the ancient "White Master".

The archaeologist should note the likenesses here to the tiger-god of the Phoenician Baal. Examples are the black-robed priesthood and the Vestal Virgins who attended the "Sacred Fire". Other similarities are to be found on both sides of the Atlantic.

THE PUANTS OR PUANS

That this was the ancient name for the mound-building Algonkins was not a discovery of the present writer. I refer to "Jesuit Relations and Allied Documents". On page 228, the statement is made by one of the exploring priests that "the ancients of the country" were known as "Puans". Note also that the "River of The Puans" is located in the Sacred Forest of Michigan. The Chippewas or Ojibways of Michigan with whom the present writer was well acquainted during college years, said the Sacred River was the Mississippi flowing to the Southern Sea (Gulf of Mexico?), and its northern source touched a spot where the headwaters also were found of a river running to the Arctic (The Northern Sea) and one to the Sunrise Sea (St. Lawrence?) as well as further west one flowing to the Sunset Sea (evidently the Columbia). This shows very interesting geographical knowledge by the ancient Puans who named these rivers "The Cross of Waters". See Chateaubriand, University of California Press.

CHEE ZOOS

Algonkin name for the Dawn-light or the Dawn-God. The Chippewas are one of the many tribes of Algonkin-tongues. This family of languages which preceded the invasion of the Siouan, Iroquoian, Muskogean and other tongues from the South up the Mississippi in waves from about 400 AD to 1000 AD, shows many Gothic words. See "Vikings and The Red Man". Here is a fascinating field for Gothic scholars.

210

INVASION OF THE SOUTHERNERS

The Serpent and Turtle (totemistic) invasion is told in Chief Deecoodah's "Traditions of Deecoodah" taken down over a hundred years ago by Walter Pidgeon in English and published. He tells how to read the Mounds. He's the last High Priest of one of the groups of Mound Builders.

It is interesting that the Siouan name for the Prophet shows that at His coming their location was probably South America. Their bringing north the domestic paw-paw (a South American plant) reinforces this lost fact. The Chippewa Chief, Black-Thunder, told the present writer that the Prophet predicted the coming of the sacrificing Serpents with their "Sacred Fire", and the coming of White Man.

SYMBOL OF THE PIERCED HAND

This is one of the signs of the Prophet throughout the Americas. In Central America it was called "The Hand Kabul" (or Kaboul). It has been found in the Spiro Mound opened by the University of Oklahoma. Also winged beings like angels were found in many mounds upon ancient pottery.

WRITING. HEBRAIC TEXT

Many of the tribes say that the Prophet taught the priesthood a secret language and writing. Could this have been Hebrew?

QUOTATION FROM PRIEST
AMERICAN ANTIQUITIES

pp 68-70 Ethan Smith related the following:

"Joseph Merrick Esq., a highly respectable character in the parish of the church at Pittsfield, gave the following account: That in 1815 he was levelling some ground under and near an old woodshed, standing on a place of his situated on "Indian Hill" (A Mound? Comment author's.). He ploughed and conveyed away many old chips and earth to some depth. After the work was done, walking over the place, he discovered, near where the earth had been dug the deepest, a black strap, as it appeared, about six inches in length, and one and one-half in breadth, and about the thickness of a leather trace to a harness. He perceived it had at each end a loop, of some hard substance, probably for the purpose of carrying it. He conveyed it to his house, and threw it into an old tool box. He afterwards found it thrown out at the door and again conveyed it to the box.

"After some time he thought he would examine it; but in attempting to cut it, found it as hard as bone; he succeeded however in breaking it open and found it was composed of two pieces of thick rawhide sewed and made water-tight with the sinews of some animal, and gummed over; and in the fold was contained four folded pieces of parchment. They were of a dark yellow hue, and contained some kind of writing. The neighbors coming in to see the strange discovery, tore one of the pieces to shreds in true Hun and Vandal style. The other three pieces Mr. Merrick saved, and sent them to Cambridge (England or Massachusetts?), where they were examined, and discovered to have been written with a pen in Hebrew, plain and legible. The writing on the three remaining pieces of parchment was quotations from the Old Testament". They were given as follows: Deut. Chap. VI from 4th to 9th verses inclusive; also Chap. XI verse 13 to 21 and Ex. Chap. XIII - 11 to 16. It is interesting in connection with the above that the small cross tattoo mark between the thumb and forefinger on Mexican and South American wild Indians is credited to the Prophet and means "Skill or good luck". The cross between the eyebrows is likewise.

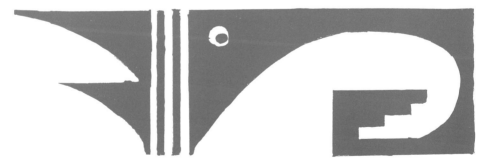

Hopi Symbol - Plumed Serpent.

MOUND BUILDER TRADE

The objects found in the mounds show extensive Central American and Mexican trade. "Plated ware" typical of pre-

Incan Chan-Chan in South America is also to be found, although not as yet identified as such. Mayan, Mexican and (probably) Chiriqui ware of Central America is common.

As for navigation, Father Mercier met Algonkins who had come 400 leagues in a fleet of canoes to trade with his party. Legends tell of ancient sea-going ships.

THE THANKSGIVING CEREMONY

This celebration which the Algonkin friends of the Pilgrims suggested as the correct way to bring in a harvest, and which the latter accepted as their own idea, is in reality a very ancient Harvest Rite going back many thousands of years into antiquity and already ancient in the time of the Prophet. Even the foods are ceremonial.

For further details see A. Hyatt Verrill's "The American Indian" and Bancroft's "Native Races".

The Ceiba (Seybo) Tree.

SACRED TREES

Throughout the Americas the oak, cedar and ceiba are considered sacred.

LAND OF PAN

The legendary homeland in the Sunrise Sea of many Indian tribes.

SHOSHONEAN NAME FOR GREAT SPIRIT

The name Wako-Naga is an interesting combination between the name of the Prophet found in South American and Naga (Lord Serpent) which is at once both Tibetan and Egyptian.

SIOUAN NAME FOR GREAT SPIRIT

The name Wah-kan is certainly that of the Prophet during His South American and Central American journeys and again underwrites the Dacotah's ancient homeland, during the time of the Prophet's coming. (The true name of the Sioux is Dacotah.)

THE SUN DANCE

This dance was cleverly analyzed by the curator of Heye Foundation Museum, New York, and anthropologist Dr. Clarke Wissler in his book "The American Indian" by making a list of all the elements of the dance and then seeking out how many were held by each tribe. He thus found that the Algonkin-speaking Arapaho had the most complete ceremony. Second place was held by the Algonkin Cree, and Siouan-speaking Dacotah was third, tying that place with the Algonkin Gros-Ventre. Thus it was apparently an Algonkin rite.

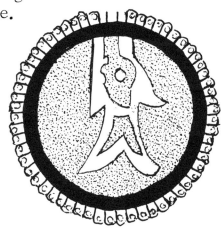

Plumed Serpent symbol worked in abalone-pearl and silver by

Indian Silversmiths, Taxco, Mexico.

THE SECRET SOCIETIES

The Meda Medicine Society was initiated by the Prophet according to legend. Algonkin informants agree. This is also true of many other tribes. It is a good field for future study. These Societies have many names, but the origin is usually given to a visit by the Prophet.

THE PLUMED SERPENT OF THE PUANS

Indian informants have agreed that the name Plumed Serpent (whether in northern United States, along the West Coast, Mexico or Central America) is always derived from the amazing control the Prophet had over the elements of wind and water. The plume symbolizes wind and the serpent is the water symbol.

THE FINDING OF THE TEN COMMANDMENTS

From Bancroft - Native Races, Vol. V, pp. 94-95. Published about 1860. Now out of print. (Quotation is from his father, A.A. Bancroft, who thus describes the discovery.)

"About eight miles southeast of Newark there was formerly a large mound composed of masses of free stone which had been brought from some distance and thrown into a heap without much placing or care. In the early days, stone being scarce in that region, the settlers carried away the Mound piece by piece to use for building purposes, so that in a few years there was little more than a large flattened heap of rubble remaining. Some fifteen years ago, the county surveyor (I have forgotten his name) who had for some time been searching ancient works, turned his attention to this particular pile. He employed a number of men and proceeded at once to open it. Before long he was rewarded by finding in the center and near the surface a bed of tough clay which must have been brought from a distance of twelve miles. This was known as pipe-clay. Imbedded in the clay was a coffin, dug out of a burr-oak log, and in a pretty good state of preservation. In the coffin was a skeleton with quite a number of stone ornaments and emblems and some open brass rings suitable for bracelets and anklets. These being removed, the men then dug deeper and discovered a stone dressed to an oblong shape of about eighteen inches long and twelve wide, which proved to be a casket, neatly fitted and entirely water-tight, containing a slab of stone of hard and fine quality, an inch and a half thick, eight inches long, four and a half wide at one end tapering to three inches at the other. Upon the face of the slab was the figure of a man, apparently a priest, with a long flowing beard and a robe reaching to his feet. Over his head was a curved line of characters, and upon the edges and back of the stone were closely and neatly carved letters. The slab, which I saw myself, was shown to the Episcopal clergyman of Newark, and he pronounced the writing to be the ten commandments in Ancient Hebrew."

Note by author: The skeleton burial of a high priest may have been within the time of white man's coming, but the so-called brass rings would be no indication of this. The Algonkins mined copper from very ancient times. In fact I was taken to such a copper mine once, blindfolded by the Chippewas, and after a long descent into the earth, allowed to look around. In the light of the torches I could see very ancient picks, they said of an alloy better than steel, although I was not allowed to touch anything. The picks resembled brass. Bancroft was himself skeptical of the ability of the clergyman to interpret the strange lettering.

THE SERI INDIANS

The legends of the Seri, a wild tribe very little touched by white contact and thoroughly pagan in belief, is a rich source of legend. It is sad that the well-meaning scientists who were able to collect these tales in their book "The Untamed Seri", did not realize that their informant would later have to pay for his betrayal of these legends with his eyesight. The Seri tribe is pitifully poverty stricken and undernourished. It is to be suspected that their steadily shrinking numbers may point to secret human sacrificial rites.

THE NAME INCAN

This has been used in the popular sense when used at all. Actually the term is a title for royalty. The name of the people is Quechua or Keechua. Translated by the Chippewa

216

(pronounced Chee-pe-hua) it means the Ancient Chee, or in Aztec, Chichimec. (Chee-chee people) When a better study has been made of Indian tongues of South America, Indian history may become much plainer. Shooting-Star of the Sioux, who was privileged to go to South America and meet some important Indian figures in the High Andes said: "Without doubt, after we exchanged the ancient secret sign of greeting, we recognized our ancient kinship. I would guess we left this land about a thousand to fifteen hundred years ago." I hope that Shooting-Star does not mind this quotation.

THE PAPAGO

The long E repetition with the S or SH sound between is found in many variations throughout the tribes and always stands for the Wind God and often for the Prophet. One high-priest interestingly corrected my pronunciation of the word Essene while speaking of the Mediterranean sect which Jesus was supposed to have been a member. "The word is" and then he repeated it, using long Es. His tone was friendly, but carried finality.

TACOBYA HOT SPRINGS AND COSO

A slumbering volcano in Inyo County California where the ancient crater holds a lake that changes its temperature from hot to boiling.

THE YAQUI

Pronounced Yah-Kee, the name according to Bancroft means "sacrificers". At present converted to Christianity, they still follow many rites of the Prophet (which incidentally are to be found throughout the Americas among the wildest jungle tribes who have never had any contact with mission-aries) such as the baptismal rite. The extent of this should be studied by some future anthropologist. It includes such similarities as godfather and godmother for life with kinship names of endearment, etcetera.

THE POWER OF THE TOLTECS

All archaeological evidence points to a far more powerful and advanced culture for the Toltec Empire than any following them. For example, the similarity of Katchina or Matchina dances, legends of trade among the Pueblo People, now isolated, throughout tribes both pagan and Christian, show equal similarities of ancient knowledge and wealth.

IRRIGATION SYSTEMS NOW LOST

Since airplanes have been flying over some of the now barren Chihuahua (ancient-ancient Che) Desert of Northern Mexico an amazing irrigation system running hundreds of miles is to be traced from the air. Hillsides of what is now the most stark wasteland must once have bloomed like a garden, bearing out ancient Yaqui legends of the fertility of the land and their own wealth in the long forgotten past. Pilots tell that some of the ancient terracing can still be seen from the air.

HOW THE PROPHET REMADE CEREMONIES

The Yaqui rite of "sacrificing fruits and flowers" upon their tables, makes one suspect the changing over of an old sacrificial ceremony by the Prophet, since the Yaqui as well as the Mayans of Central America credit the Prophet with this rite. One wonders if the child baptismal so often credited to the Prophet was not a child-sacrifice before the coming of "The Pale One"; or the dances were not olden ceremonies which He changed rather than strictly forbidding what was evidently an integral part of their culture pattern.

From the Pascolas of the Yaqui, through the Katchinas of the Hopi, and the Katsanas of the other Pueblos, to similar dances throughout Mexico and South America one sees an ancient pattern undoubtedly much older than the coming of Kate-Zahl, because often the dancing leader or supervisor or gobernador is the figure of the Fire-God already ancient when the pyramids of Egypt were first built, and any Egyptologist would recognize parts of the rites and the names. However, where the "Gobernador" is gowned in white and bearded, many parts of the rites are changed. The two clowns are almost always retained with

218

their rather robust humor, and yet in the entire rite there is a difference. In the Mexican Mountain Region, in the dance of the Turahumaras, the figure of the "Monarcho" wears a pale mask and a beard, while in the Brazilian jungles the leader is as much the black-masked Fire-God as in the Apache Crown Dance of Arizona. The colors of the Fire-God incidentally are black and red, the shades of lava when hot and cold.

THE CITY OF TULA

That I may neither be accused of absurd exaggeration by those not acquainted with Indian legends concerning the Toltec Capitol, nor on the other hand of slavish plagiarism by those versed in the Toltec book "Song of Quetzalcoatl" translated from the Aztec by Dr. John Hubert Cornyn of Mexico University, I admit my indebtedness to both sources. Even the four-beat trochee cadence of the Toltec relic, meant to be chanted as Indian sagas are, beat itself into my mind while trying to write the story of the Prophet, until I gave up and placed the tale in its ancient setting. That the same beat was used for a Finnish saga, which incidentally I have never had the pleasure of reading, is incidental.

This fact can be proved by the Song of Hiawatha. When I was "adopted" during a college vacation into the Chippewa Tribe of Michigan, I immediately thought of "From the land of the Ojibway, From the Land of Hiawatha." The Indians looked at me in amazement. They had never heard of Hiawatha. True, the words were theirs, although mispronounced. For example "Nokomis" meaning "my grandmother", as "KoKomis" means "my grandfather" (a term of great respect and endearment), are Ojibway (now spelled as pronounced Chippewa), but the accent is on the last syllable. Gitche-Gumee brought laughter. I finally learned the name was Kitchee-Gaumee, for Big-Sea-Water. They listened with great interest. The rhythm intrigued them. That was very Indian; it was the beat of all their sagas, and many of their dances. But WHO was Hiawatha? The nearest meaning was Hee-ah-whasa, or Very-Far-Off. They themselves then suggested the solution of the mystery. The Saga was that of another Indian tribe, but the setting was their woodland. Could it be that the writer, being a white man and needing Indian words, used Bishop Barraga's dictionary of what he called the "Ojibway language? I looked it up when I returned to college. The dates matched. Longfellow must have used the Barraga Dictionary. But then from what tribe came the original story, or did he just make it up. It had quite an Indian understanding for an invented tale!

The answer came several years later, and not from any puzzled English professors. I had asked members of tribe after tribe. I circulated among the extras at Hollywood where many men and women of various tribes make a living. Finally I thusly met tall, handsome Big-Tree, a Seneca Indian from New York State. At the mention of the name Hiawatha, his face lit up as if an electric light had been turned on from within.

"He is our great tribal hero. Once when we were chanting his saga, Longfellow was among our guests."

Big Tree, a Seneca, tells that the story of Hiawatha is two Seneca legends intertwined by Longfellow.

"Longfellow did not get it quite right, but we honor him for his beautiful saga; so Indian in its feeling. Every year we pay him eternal tribute; we have a ritualistic dance in his honor."

Which is indeed an honor very few white men can claim! If white scholars can ever get Indians to chant these sagas, more will be uncovered in the future, and I am certain the beat will be in the ancient trochee.

THE ANCIENT CHANT

It must be remembered when reading the "Song of Quetzalcoatl" that this Toltec saga has come down through two enemy tongues of conquering nations which have added bits and comments of their own. Both the Chichimecs and the Aztecs were dominated by the sacrificing Priesthood which had been fought by the Prophet and were routed from the churches. When the Aztecs returned the bloody priesthood to power, they still had a tremendous fear of the power of the "White God" and they gave him a temple outside their own pantheon; but they were not above poking sly ridicule in his direction.

Pyramid of the Sun at San Juan, Teotihuacan.

THE SITE OF TULA

This is a much debated question among Mexican archaeologists. The town with its ruins upon the hill overlooking the valley is hardly extensive enough for the Toltec capitol, even though it carries the name of Tula. According to the Indian tribe, the name has differed from Tollan to Tulan, but in the main the description is the same. Dr. Cornyn, translator of the legend, favors the site at Teotihuacan, and since I have been to Mexico and have seen both sites, I could not agree more fully, especially since carbon-dating has taken from the extensive ruins of Teotihuacan the absurd "built just before the conquest" ideas of certain anthropologists who would impose their iron-clad views upon archaeology, returned to the site its two millenia to two and a half millenia date. Cornyn's description of the site in his Notes is worth quoting.

"Under the ruined city of Teotihuacan lie the ruins of a much earlier civilization buried beneath fifteen to twenty feet of debris washed down from the surrounding hills. Vast underground stairways of soft conglomerate stone faced with

221

cement take us to underground chambers of the fire-worshippers who preceded the lava flows which inundated the southern end of the valley.

"On the ruins of this long-dead metropolis arose Tula of early Nahuatl times. Through the city an avenue several miles in length runs which was lined with temples. On the north it terminated in the temple-studded wall inclosing the Grand Court of the Pyramid of the Moon. Southwest it passed in front of the Shrine of Quetzal-coatl. Midway between these extremes stood the Pyramid of the Sun, raising its bulk above the conglomeration of temples, palaces and shrines.

"No deity had a greater shrine than Quetzal-coatl. A vast court over six hundred feet wide by nineteen hundred feet long surrounded by a massive wall two hundred and sixty feet thick at the base and thirty two feet high, crowned by fifteen minor temples rising from all four sides bore witness to the reverence the Toltecs paid to their greatest and most revered deities. The famous wall of Babylon dwarfs into insignificance in the presence of this vast sanctuary erected more than ten centuries ago to the God-Of-The-Winds. Along the top of its wall, over a mile in length, a score of horses might race abreast or a hundred thousand spectators of ceremonials, games, songs or dances might have seated themselves.

"In the center of the court on a truncated pyramid is a ceremonial altar reached on all sides by stairs containing the thirteen traditional steps representing the thirteen cycles ·of The-First-Sun-Age. In the rear of this altar stands a higher one approached by a single stairway of thirty-nine steps, symbolical of the thirty-nine Ages."

(At this point one remembers the history books which were thrown into the flames by the conquering Spanish.)

THE ANCIENT NAME TEOTIHUACAN

Some natives living near the grounds of the museum at the ruins crowded around the University students, and when I found one who could speak English I succeeded in getting an answer to a burning question: "What does Teo-ti mean?"

"Teo means God in Nahuatl and Ti means city. The name

222

stands for: The city of the God Wahcan."

That is when I knew that this indeed was Tula!

Unfortunately the ruins have never been excavated except by dozens of children who are busy day and night digging out artifacts to sell to the tourists.

TULA DANCES

I learned that the Prophet is credited with introducing chanting and answering choruses sometimes from mountain to mountain, in his revision of the rituals.

THE WHITE WAR-GOD

This figure, apparently a Viking by his Nordic features, led the early Aztecs into battle. Willard in his book "The Bearded Conqueror" continually confuses him with the earlier Prophet and calls the Aztec warriors with their typical head-dress or warbonnet so similar to the Sioux, Toltecs. In spite of these errors the book is full of interest.

THE VENUS CALENDAR

This method of telling time is probably vastly older than the century of the Prophet. However, that it was used by the Pale One so often, it is well that it is at least partially understood. As a method of time-reckoning it is used from the north of North America to the south of South America, or was used before The Conquest. Sometimes its numbers are known only, and Venus referred to as "The Star Boys" or "Twin-Star God" showing a degeneration of ancient knowledge.

Venus, being the second planet from the Sun and Earth the third, swings around its internal orbit making thirteen revolutions to eight revolutions of the Earth. Thus among all Indian tribes the Earth-number is eight, and the number of the Morning and Evening Star (depending on time of year viewed) is thirteen. Eight thirteens then would bring the planets into their original position. This would be a full cycle, or one hundred and four years. A half cycle would be fifty two years. Upon this most American Indian reckoning is based. However, it is often checked by other reckoning. The Mayans have four inter-revolving calendars - one like ours, the Sun-year and its 1/4 day which is comparatively simple - the Moon, etcetera. I would not suggest that anyone study the Mayan calendrical system unless he has a major in mathematics and a minor in astronomy. It makes for pretty stiff studying when the mathematics is to be translated on a twenty basis instead of the ten we use, and then each number is a different god in various positions. The Mayans wrote a date usually four times. They were well acquainted with the weight and measurement of the earth, the swing of the sun from Capricorn to Cancer and back, the Precession of the Equinoxes and the fact that our Sun is moving through space, carrying our family of planets along. They believed the Sun is circumnavigating a Central Fire located in the Heavens near the Pleiades which they called Mya. (This is the way their name is pronounced.) On many of their great stone stele, which the Spanish were unable to destroy, we are able to read the dates, but the events thus far are still a mystery. The dates are of themselves fascinating, a few going back into fantastic antiquity. Perhaps some day we shall learn what happened on these dates.

THE SACRED CITY

The great pyramid of Cholula is estimated to have covered forty to forty-five acres, and though not as high as Egypt's Cheops, yet has a larger base. From the pen of Bernal Diaz, one of the Spanish conquerors, we have this description of the ancient city at the time of the Conquest.

"The city at that time had above a hundred lofty white towers which were the temples of their idols, one of which was held in special veneration."

This was undoubtedly the pyramid of the Prophet. The

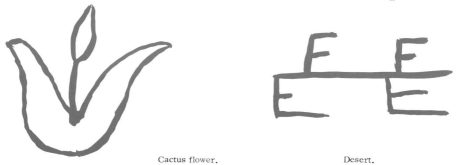

Cactus flower.   Desert.

Aztecs would never have touched it, although regarding it as beyond their own pantheon. Because of the predictions of their coming doom, they looked upon this pyramid with fear.

With the Spanish it was different. They tried their best to demolish it, and then wearying of their Herculean task, merely covered up the entire pyramid with rubble and built a church on top. This was not built, however, until after they found out that the people still took their sick to the new top of the pyramid for a blessing. Therefore they called the church The Shrine of Healing.

THE GROVE OF TULE
The tree of this legend, located in Oaxaca (pronounced Wah-ha-ca) still lives. It is the largest living thing in The Americas and probably the world. Also it is probably the oldest. Ten feet above the ground, it has a circumference of over ninety feet (It takes 26 men holding hands to circle it). It is a cypress or American Cedar.

THE PROPHET'S MANTLE
The Ceiba or "the silk-cotton tree" is sacred to the memory of the Prophet in many small Mexican towns. There were legends of mantles reposing at this or that shrine at the time of the Conquest but they have long since disappeared. The Ceiba also attains great age and there are several in Mexico supposed to have been blessed by the Prophet.

THE PROPHET TRAVELS THE COUNTRY
George Squier in his book "Peru" describes a massive temple to the Prophet whom they call Vira Cocha. It was built around an artificial lake and dominated by a great statue of the Healer in a white toga reaching to his feet. A chained tiger was following him.

More legends of South America on the subject of the Prophet are contained in Bancroft. Wild animals lay down and rolled before Him and everywhere is mentioned His ability to walk on water. Further references are Central and South American Books, by Hewett. Memorias Antiguas Historiales del Peru, by Fernando Montesinos. Recherches de Chili, by Warden.

225

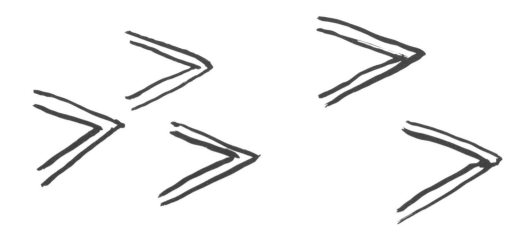

The trail of the Great One.

FURTHER STUDY ON THE PROPHET

There are an amazing number of Christian words used in the ritualistic practices of the pagan Mayans far back in the jungles unknown to any white men except those who have accepted the Mayan religion and have been taken to the ancient shrines. Such words are sin, Trinity, Virgin Birth of Prophet, etc. Any reader interested is referred to: Documentos Ineditos Relaciones de Yucatan. This amazing volume was compiled shortly after the Conquest.

Other interesting books are: Historia Apologetica, by Las Casas (a saintly monk who did not approve of what he was forced to observe, and who suspected a mystery in the legends he heard.) Mexican Antiquities, by Kingsborough (who also suspected a mystery). Archaeological Studies, by Brasseur de Bourbourg. Long Ago Told, by H.B. Wright. The Traditions of Deecoodah, as told to Walter Pidgeon, published by Sampson Low and Sons, London, 1853. All five volumes of Bancroft are a mine of legend and sources now lost.

THE MOUND BUILDERS

The Mound Builders, who according to carbon-dating were flourishing at the beginning of the Christian Era, were, with little doubt, the Algonkin-speaking North Ameri-

226

can Indian. The only truly authentic book which has come down to our time is "Traditions of Decoodah" taken down by a young surveyor during the forties of the last century and published in London, England over a hundred years ago.

When the young surveyor took his instruments, a bed blanket and a gun into the wilderness west of St. Louis to map the contours of the mounds, he found his camp visited by a dignified old man who watched his work with interest.

| Turtle. | Ship. | Circle. |

Symbols of the Turtle.

Later, through an interpreter, he was asked why he desired to map the mounds while his people were so busy tearing them down? His reply, that he wished to bridge the time of the destroyers to another age when someone not yet born would find them of great interest, brought a thoughtful nod from his visitor. He was invited to the Indian camp and there found that he had been entertaining Dee-coo-dah, last High Priest of the Elk Nation who had intended to take the history of his lost people to the grave since his sons had all been killed in battle and his tribe was extinct. However, young Pidgeon persuaded him to change his mind and tried to learn the old man's language for better communication.

During the next four months, the aged high-priest led young Pidgeon to many of the greatest mounds, often explaining the original contours before erosion by streams or rivers. At last, satisfied at the young white man's true interest, Dee-coo-dah began to explain how the mounds could be read, since they were actually historical. The writing was from the inside out, and when a dynasty had been ended, it was marked by the "mound-of-extinction". That Pidgeon did not get as much information as he might have is certainly due to his fumbling grasp of the Algonkin language. However, in spite of its short-comings, the book is a mine of

"The Tortoise crosses water".

information, as yet almost undiscovered by modern archaeologists and universities since the book is now out of print and very rare.

Dee-coo-dah's discussion of the Puan Capitol, and the "Sacred city" at the "Great Cross of Waters" in the Michigan-Wisconsin area whose history ran ninety-six dynasties terminating after the Civil-War of the Serpent Invaders; the descriptions of the Court life of the Black Tortoise Emperor at the site of the old Puan Capitol after the Turtle-Snake invasion from the south up the Mississippi, proved for the present writer to be the Rosetta Stone to Ancient American History. Suddenly, curious animal legends began to take on meanings (and the whole weird picture-puzzle of the anthropologists at present still possessed with the sole and recent Asian entrance theories of Hrdlicka) began to take on a new aspect of history which explains not only the strange (and for white-man, meaningless) animal stories, but also the language maps.

With but a few western exceptions, the Algonkin-speaking people once ruled the entire North American continent above the Mexican border, extending from the Atlantic into Arizona and California. They were a trading people, as is evidenced by materials and jewelry found in the mounds. Their empire was built on trade and peace. It was a well ordered empire with a Christ-like religion, brought in by the White Prophet with well established temples and ritual.

The empire came to an end after the invasion of the Fire-worshipping Turtle and Serpent (invading from the south) had partially overthrown the southern portion. However an uneasy peace continued for several generations until a young Captain named Dacotah grew up in the court of the Black Tortoise and began to intrigue with the

228

Northern Puans. After establishing himself with Puan help as Emperor over the Serpent-Tortoise Empire, another period of peace continued until the time of Dacotah's grandson. Dacotah was engaged in consolidating his gains in the west and had as his goal one solid empire from sea to sea. His grandson, coming of age in the southern court of his son, was able to unite the Serpents in a rebellion against the northern Tortoise. This occurred at the time of tremendous invasions of the Athapascan-speaking tribes from Asia down the west coast, and when the western lands were in turmoil. Civil war on the Mississippi then followed, and at last anarchy. The date of this was about 1,000 A.D., or several centuries before the coming of Columbus. The years of invasion of war and turmoil were evidently from the Seventh Century on.

In the language picture, the Siouan tongues were those of the Black Tortoise leading the Snakes. The latter people were the Iroquois, Caddoan and Muskogean-speaking tongues extending down the Mississippi to the Natchez, now extinct, whose legends told to early explorers completely confirm this sequence of events.

During the early part of the Christian Era when the Puan Empire was strong and vigorous, it must have been in close touch with Central Mexico, or the Tula of that day; the Chorotegans to the South of Mexico; and perhaps even on to ancient Chan-Chan in Peru. Similar types of metal-working seems to suggest some kind of trade connection.

The great hollow-log with many-rowers fleet of the Puan is described by various early explorers. Of course, the Serpent tongues, evidently stemming from the direction of the Caribbean Sea to the Amazon, were also at home on water with similar ships.

THE GREAT MOUNDS OF ST. LOUIS

The descriptions of Puan Cities is a combination of legends and the descriptions of early explorers. The strawberry carpet was used by many tribes.

The Mounds, first of the Puans and then of the conquering Serpents (who merely added to the conquered city without ravaging same), came down to the early Nineteenth

Century. The grandfather of the present writer, who was born and raised in St. Louis, spoke of these Mounds. I do not remember if he was a personal witness or heard about it from his mother, but the story is that some speculators from the eastern United States, probably New York, bought up the land, and then excavated them with no thought of historical sequence, selling the "trinkets" found therein for what they would bring among curiosity seekers. Some of the work was of copper, some of the jewelry of silver, and a few exquisite pieces of gold. He said that there were old yellowed sheets of some kind of parchment with strange writings and pottery depicting what looked like angels, as well as numerous other interesting bowls. There were stones sewn on what had been cloth: such as pearls, turquoise, jade, obsidian and what he later thought might have been emeralds.

Asked if there had been a white garment like a man's toga with black crosses around the hem-line, he hesitated and said:

"I couldn't say for certain. There were so many, many things. Some air-tight boxes fashioned of metal and even of worked stone had been broken open. Such a garment would have been discarded as valueless, I am certain."

TRADE BETWEEN MEXICO AND PERU IN PRE-INCAN TIMES

There are several facts which suggest Pre-Incan Toltec-Zapotec-trade with the Kingdoms of Chan-Chan and that of the Nascas of Peru. (Both the latter nations were finally submerged by the rising power of the Incas.)

First there is the matter of the colored cotton. While it was but a legend in Mexico, and until recently regarded with great amusement, it was a reality in Peru. Dr. Harrington, Curator of the Southwest Indian Museum of Los Angeles, California, told the present writer in 1955 that scientific tests upon the magnificent textile work found upon Pre-Incan Peruvian mummies proved that the colored cotton was indeed a reality.

Next there is the matter of plating and unusual metal work in jewelry. Magnificent examples of the first have been found in the ruins of Chan-Chan, although they remain but a legend in Mexico. Probably they did come down to the time of the Spanish Conquest when so much gold and silver was melted down by the conquerors. A few pieces of lovely gold work have been found in the ruins of Monte Alban now being uncovered by the Mexican Government.

Finally there is the matter of the Nasca vases recently found in Mexico. One of the Nasca cat-faced design was uncovered in the Monte Alban ruins. In almost any archaeological site in the world this would be accepted as evidence of trade. Early scientists noted the likeness between the designs of Mitla Mexico and those of Chan-Chan. In both cases, textile designs were the inspiration for stone work of a similar and beautiful type. Squier says of the Mound Builders: "Of the pottery, various though not abundant specimens of their skill have been recorded, which in elegance of model, delicacy and finish, as also in fineness of material, come fully up to the best Peruvian specimens, to which they bear, in many respects, a close resemblance." Also speaking of the Mound Builder art in pottery, Bancroft says: "Nearly every beast, bird and reptile indigenous to the country is truthfully represented, together with some creatures now only found in tropical climates, such as the lamantin and toucan."

ADDITIONAL NOTES ON MOUND BUILDERS
(Quoted from Bancroft)
"The Great Mississippi Valley system of ancient works consisting of mounds and embankments of earth and stone, erected by the race known as the Mound Builders, extends over a territory bounded in general terms as follows: on the north by the Great Lakes, on the east by New York, Pennsylvania and Virginia, in the east but farther south extending to the Atlantic Coast and including Florida, Georgia and a part of South Carolina; on the south by the Gulf of Mexico, including Texas; on the west by an indefinite line extending from Lake Superior through Minnesota, Nebraska, Kansas and Indian Territory (Oklahoma), although there are some reported remains farther west, particularly on the upper Missouri which have not been thoroughly explored."

(Since the time when this was written, pilots have reported Giant Mounds throughout the west, particularly Arizona, and extending down through the Chihuahua Valley.)

"The works of the Mound Builders are almost exclusively confined to the fertile valleys still best fitted to support a dense population. The Mississippi and its tributaries have, during the progress of the centuries, worn down their valleys in three or four successive terraces, which, except the lowest or the latest formed, the ancient peoples chose as the site of their structures. They gave preference in rearing their grandest cities (for cities there must have been) to the terrace plains near the junction of the larger streams."

* * *

"The total number of Mounds in the State of Ohio (alone) is estimated by the best authority at ten thousand, while the enclosures were at least fifteen hundred."

(Comment: In the year 1961 there would not be many left.)

Typical of numerous descriptions by Bancroft is the following: "The work shown in the next cut is part of a group in Pike County, Ohio. The circle is three hundred feet in diameter." He goes on to show a perfect square within it, perfectly oriented to the cardinal points, apparently for star observation. Another is described as follows (he is speaking of temple mounds or pyramids and this one is at Cahokia, Illinois): "Its base measures seven hundred feet by five hundred feet. The height is ninety feet. On one end above the mid height is a terrace platform one hundred and sixty by three hundred and fifty feet or nearly two acres - the base covering five acres."

* * *

"The bases assume a variety of forms, square, rectangular, octagonal, round, oval etcetera, but the curves and angles are always extremely regular."

* * *

"Mr. Dickeson speaks confidently of gold, silver, galena and copper money left by the Mound Builders."

* * *

"The temple mounds resemble in their principal features the Southern Pyramids; at least they imply a likeness of religious ideas in the builders. The use of obsidian implements shows a connection, either through origin, war, or commerce with the Mexican nations, or at least with nations who came in contact with the Nahuas."

(Comment: today this does not mean exclusively the Aztec, but the earlier Toltec and kindred groups speaking the Nahuatl family of languages.)

* * *

"The works were not built by a migrating people, but by a race that lived long in the land. It seems unlikely that the results attained could have been accomplished in less than four or five centuries. Nothing indicates that the time did not extend to thousands of years, but it is only respecting the minimum time that there can be any grounds for reasonable conjecture. If we suppose the civilization indigenous, of course a much longer period must be assigned to its development than if it was introduced by a migration - or

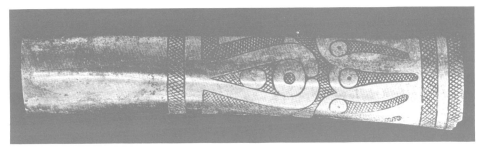

Carved human femur, Hopewell Mounds.

rather a colonization, for civilized and semi-civilized peoples do not migrate en masse. Moreover a northern origin would imply a longer duration of time than one from the south, where a degree of civilization is known to have existed.

"How long a time has elapsed since the Mound Builders abandoned their works? Here again a minimum estimate only can be sought. No work is more enduring than an embankment of earth. There is no positive internal proof that they were not standing one, five, or ten thousand years ago. The evidences of an ancient abandonment of the works, or serious decline of the builder's power, are as follows: first the fact that none of them stand on the last-formed terrace of the rivers, while most on the oldest terrace,

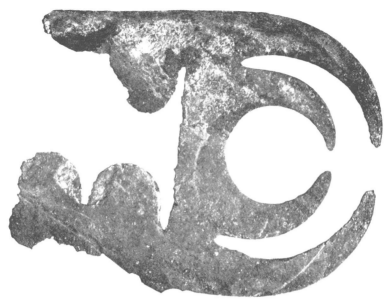
Serpent head design in copper, Hopewell Mounds.

and that those on the second bear in some cases marks of having been invaded by water. The rate of terrace-forming varies on different streams and there are no sufficient data for estimating in years the time required for the formation of any one of the terraces; at least scientific men are careful not to give a definite opinion in the matter, but it is evident that each required a very long period, and the last one a much longer time than any of the others, on account of the gradual longitudinal leveling of the river-beds. Second, the complete disappearance of all wooden structures, which must have had great solidity. Third, the advanced state of decomposition of human bones in a soil well calculated for their preservation. Skeletons found in Europe are well preserved at a known age of eighteen hundred years. Fourth, the absence of Mound Builders from the traditions of modern tribes."

(Comment: this inability of Bancroft to have made contact with the modern tribes was one of his greatest weaknesses. By the term "contact" or "making contact" the modern anthropologist means a man's ability to learn from the ancient nations. Some learned men admittedly lack this important ability. The Red Man being questioned either turns his back or simply answers "yes" to every-thing. Result - nothing.)

234

Fifth, the fact that the mounds were covered in the seventeenth century with primitive forests, uniform with those which covered the other parts of the country. In this latitude the age of a forest tree may be much more accurately determined than in tropical climates; and trees from four hundred to five hundred years old have been examined by many well-authenticated cases over mounds and embankments. Equally large trees in all stages of decomposition were found at their feet, either on or under the ground, so that the abandonment of the work must be dated back at least twice the actual age of the standing trees. It is a fact well known to woodsmen that when cultivated land is abandoned, the first growth is very unlike the original forest, both in the species and size of the trees, and that several generations would be required to restore the primitive timber. Consequently a thousand years must have passed since some of the works were abandoned. The monuments of the Mississippi present stronger internal evidence of antiquity than any others in America, although it by no means follows that they are older than Palenque and Copan. The height of the Mound Builders' power should not, without very positive external evidence, be placed at a later date than the fifth or sixth century of our era."

* * *

I have quoted Bancroft at length because his volumes are very difficult to obtain, being long out of print, and because on the whole he tries to be conservative and scientific. He had the help of vast volumes which are at present entirely unobtainable and therefore his studies are not to be taken lightly. He is, in fact, more scientific in his approach than a few of our modern scientists, who failing to make contact, are more inspired by their prejudices than by deduction from facts. For example, the following is dis-

Obsidian blades from altar.

235

counted by Bancroft although to the present writer interesting because similar in type to the miniature found in Mound Builder territory. Bancroft is speaking about ruins found in the vicinity of Panuco, Mexico. He is quoting, and speaking about Norman's Rambles by Land and Water, pp. 145-51, 164 and 149-50, at present unobtainable.

"West of the (ruined) town five or six mounds from 30 to 40 feet high are vaguely mentioned. Buried in the ground in a ravine near the town, and resting on the stone walls of a dilapidated sepulchre, Mr. Norman claims to have found a stone slab seven feet long, wider at one end than the other, but two feet and a half in average width, one foot thick, and bearing on one side the sculptured figure of a man. Dressed in a flowing robe, with girdle, sandal ties on his feet, and a close fitting cap on his head, he lies with crossed arms. The face is Caucasian in feature, and the work is very perfectly executed. For the authenticity of so remarkable a relic, Mr. Norman is hardly a sufficient authority. San Nicolas, five leagues and Trinidad six leagues south-west of Panuco, are other places where ruins are reported to exist."

The foregoing from Hubert H. Bancroft Vol. 4, Antiquities. The Set is entitled Native Races of North America. Published 1875. D. Appleton and Company, New York, N.Y., printed by H.O. Houghton, Riverside, Cambridge. Very difficult to obtain. Long out of print.

THE SENECA LEGEND

This Algonkin legend was first collected by the early explorers who were able to gather legends much more easily than the present day scientists, since white men have often ridiculed these legends which they do not understand, and the key to which they do not hold.

However, the author first heard of it from Big-Tree of the Seneca during the twenties and at that time was filed away in memory as another strange white-Prophet legend due perhaps to early missionary contact. This, of course, was refuted by finding very early repetitions of the legend during recent research among old books and it is therefore included. (It was told to me merely as an illustration that the tallest men are not always the greatest. Big-Tree was about six-feet-two. I have no idea of his age, for when the Indian lives in the open, he ages slowly, and retains his hair color and all of his teeth in sound condition until the nineties.)

If Big-Tree is still alive, I am certain that he will not object to the inclusion of this lovely legend.

THE WEARING OF EAGLE FEATHERS

An eagle feather worn in the hair by a warrior denotes that he has been decorated by the tribe for bravery. The bravest deed, or the one the most respected, is the striking of a fully-armed opponent with the coup-stick (a sacred wand decorated with certain feathers), and riding away without drawing a weapon of any kind.

ABSTENTION FROM WAR WHILE THE

It is a very well known fact that the American Indian will not make war while the Morning Star is shining. The United States Military have long known this, having been told the fact by their own Indian scouts, and having learned by experience of its veracity.

THE AMERICAN INDIAN AS A WARRIOR

The United States Military today grudgingly admits that the American Indian is without doubt the greatest warrior upon the face of the planet. If there are any challenges to this statement, let them put the feats of their favorites against these facts of history. In each case these warriors were outnumbered from fifty to five hundred to one, and besides were burdened by caring for their women and children who followed them on the war-trail.

Mangus-Colorado of the Mimembres-Apaches, and his son Cochise of the Chiricawa-Apaches, as well as Geronimo of the Mescallero-Apaches all fought for many years throughout Arizona and New Mexico as well as Old Mexico. Cochise fought for sixteen years and finally gave up and agreed to go to a reservation when he was allowed to keep his land and choose his own Indian Agent, a white man he

237

knew to be honest. He kept the peace until his death, when his people were moved to less desirable land.

Geronimo fought bitterly with every means fair and foul he could command for his people. He had only fourteen to seventeen warriors, besides women and children, and held off two armies, the United States and Mexican, for over fourteen years. He was finally captured under the white flag as was Mangus-Colorado. The treachery of capturing an enemy under the white flag was resorted to when all other means had apparently failed. Mangus-Colorado was shot and Geronimo placed in prison for many years, but finally sent to the Arizona-New Mexico location of all Apache reservations.

Chiefs Little-Wolf and Dull-Knife of the Cheyennes gave up their cold mountainous lands in Wyoming and agreed to be placed on a reservation in Oklahoma. There the terrific heat, to which the Cheyennes were unaccustomed, together with lack of food due to graft in the administration of the reservation, caused great hardship. Such childhood diseases as measles killed thousands since the Indians had little white-corpuscle resistance built up throughout the ages to disease. There had been no disease before the coming of the Europeans.

Under these intolerable conditions, two chiefs of these proud people agreed to try to get back to their own land. Chief Dull-Knife, a fine philosophical man, agreed to take most of the older people and the smallest children. Little-Wolf took the most vigorous of both sexes and the older children. Making themselves bows and arrows, they set off through almost the entire width of the United States with Montana as their goal. At one point they had to cross a wide swift-flowing river with the bank filled by the camps of the Army which was determined to stop them and turn them back. Dull-Knife, almost within sight of his homeland, was surrounded, and after wretched days of misery, was gunned down to the last human being.

Little-Wolf broke through every trap the Army had set and finally reached Montana and the high mountains. Then the Army, realizing that it would be almost impossible to dislodge him, agreed to let him choose his own reservation

238

and remain. That is why today there are two reservations for the Cheyenne - the Northern and the Southern. This story is interestingly told in the book "The Last Frontier".

Chief Joseph of the Oregon Nez Perce woodland people had always been at peace with the incoming settlers. They were a fine intelligent group, many of whom had married among the whites. When investors desired to obtain the land, the Government sent Chief Joseph an order to move to an unknown location. When his scouts told the Nez Perce that the land was utterly undesirable with little chance for earning a living, Chief Joseph took his entire band of hitherto unwarlike people - men, women and children - through the mountains all the way to Canada with the entire Army in pursuit. He escaped trap after trap and even set a few himself.

He was captured a few miles from the Canadian border after a 72-day retreat only because he had been informed that he had crossed the international boundary, and therefore allowed his band to rest without posting the usual guard. When those who were left of his people after the cannonading had stopped finally raised the white flag and agreed to go with the soldiers to the reservation for which they had been intended, the spirit of the great Chief was broken. At the reservation, in the heat where the injured were dying like flies of strange diseases, Joseph said sadly: "We have prayed to the Great Spirit, but for the Nez Perce He has been looking the other way."

The Sioux, whose tribal name is Dacotah, were finally allowed to keep their reservation in their ancestral Dacotas only because of their fighting ability. It was simply too difficult to dislodge them.

This was the same in the case of many other tribes. Naturally when the tragedy of those who had agreed to move, and whose agony - such as the Creeks, Choctah, Cherokee and Chicasaw treks from the Southern States to Oklahoma (as told in "The Trail of Tears") reached the other tribes, this made them unwilling to give up ancestral lands.

Most of the battles which were won by the Army over the tribes was due to scouts and the help of friendly tribes.

Today the embryo generals in West Point study the military problems which these Indian leaders found and how they met these problems. The United States Army has at last recognized that these men of the last century, wearing eagle feathers in their hair, were certainly to be listed among the greatest military strategists upon the entire planet.

* * *

In World War I the Sioux say that they used to crawl through the German lines every dark night and get apples to sell. When I asked some white Americans stationed with them, if the Sioux had apples they answered: "Yes, they did. They told the officers that they were sharing tribes-men's fruit which came through the mail, but that is an unlikely story, for our own fruit sent to us seldom got through, and they always had apples. We often wondered."

* * *

In World War II, when General Patton arrived to look over the raw Indian recruits whom he was organizing into the Thunderbird Batallion, he strode up to the Indian Officer-of- the -Day in a fury:

"I have been over the grounds from one end to the other, and no one even challenged me!"

Whereupon two Indians materialized from some nearby trees. One spoke up: "We know, sir. We have been following you."

THE INDIAN AS A CONSERVATIONIST

The Indian tribes as a whole were very conservative about food animals. None were killed needlessly, and with the buffalo, every part of the animal was used. The Sioux, who saved the great American bison from extinction by saving four calves who were lost when the American hide hunters were slaughtering the herds and leaving the bodies to rot, are very careful about their herd today.

In Real West Magazine for July 1960, Carlton Mays has this to say about the disappearance of the buffalo: "In 1871 when Gen. Sheridan, seeing the great herds diminish, asked Washington for the power to stop the slaughter, President Grant refused to approve the order. The reason was simple, if brutal. As long as the buffalo roamed the prairies in large numbers, the Indians could carry on an endless war. With the buffalo, their food and life, gone, the Indians were helpless. So the order went out from Washington to encourage the slaughter of the buffalo."

Concerning other hunting, the religion of most tribes demands that the hunter first dance for the soul of the animals to be killed, explaining food needs. This custom, they say was instituted by the Prophet.

THE INDIAN AS A FIRE FIGHTER

Indians are used very widely as fire-fighters, throughout the Western States. As soon as a fire goes out of control, either Zuni, Hopi, Apache, Navaho or some other tribe is flown to the area. Why? Once in Beaumont, when the San Gabriel Mountains were blazing like a giant torch in 1953, I sat down at a lunch counter beside two tired fire-fighters, and from their conversation I received my answer. It began with the waitress who came over to refill their coffee cups.

"Well boys, I hear you will be soon going home. The Apaches arrived a couple of days ago, and they tell me already the main hot-spots are cold."

"Yep," one answered with a grin. "After they do their mumbo-jumbo, the fire goes down."

As the girl walked away laughing, the other man said:

"Call it mumbo-jumbo if you want, but nothing short of a miracle stopped that furnace, and you know what did it? Some marks on a few trees."

"What? You're joking."

"No, I am not. It's got me beat and I can't help thinking about it."

"How do you know?"

"Jack told me. He said that the Old-Man met the Chief and was given orders to place us along one side while the Apaches would take the other. The big line of the furnace was not tended because the Apaches had 'put their marks on the trees'. So what happened to the main line? I ask you, what happened?"

"Well the fire sort of died down."

"That's right. It did not pass the marks! Call it mumbo-jumbo if you wish, but neither of us could do the same, and for my money, they can do all the hokus-pokus they want if they can make a holocaust like that one lie down and say 'Uncle!' ''

* * *

On November 6, 1961 a fire broke out in the exclusive Belaire district of North Hollywood. Before it was contained one week later it had swept to the sea, taking with it some of the most beautiful foliage and most expensive estates in Southern California. Altogether some five hundred homes were destroyed. The local firemen made a tremendous stand against the holocaust. The local television station showed one man standing under a hundred foot tongue of flame, shoveling dirt off of a cliff into the furnace. The Indians were not called, perhaps because it was a local fire under city authorities.

One week later a second fire broke out in Tijunga Canyon and after burning up ten homes headed for the National Forest through three canyons on a wide front. The terrain being quite inaccessible at this point, Indians were flown in. The fire was out within thirty-six hours.

PRONUNCIATIONS OF INDIAN NAMES

Sioux is pronounced Soo; Cheyenne is Shy-Ann; Alleghenies is Ally-gay-nees and Cochise is Coh-chees. Hopi is Hope-ee.

LOCATION OF PUANT CAPITOL

See Traditions of Deecoodah, translated by Walter Pidgeon from the Algonkin language.

WOVEN COTS

The author has slept in these cots made by the Chippewas. Branches of the pine and cedar are woven to form a bed and the whole is padded with moss. They are very comfortable.

NOTES ON THE HAVA SUPAI LEGENDS

When Tocobya The Prophet with His staff and white mantle came down the trail named after Him, He found the Mohave, Paiutes, Havasupai and the Walapai quarreling over the land.

242

He sent the Mohave west, the Paiutes north, the Havasu to the east and the Walapai to the mesas south of Colorado.

Among the customs which He instituted was the use of the seat-lodge to be followed by a cold plunge in the water. This lodge is called the Toholwa.

THE CALENDARS

It is to be noted that the Prophet Kate-Zahl used the Venus Calendar for his computations. This is true in almost all tribal computing of any length in all the Americas, although often in the wild tribes the meaning of the numbers is either secret or has been lost. For example, Venus is spoken of as the Double-star (dawn star part of the year and evening star during the rest), but the number given in all cases is thirteen.

In Mayan computations, there are four inter-revolving calendars: 1) The sun-year of 365 1/4 days which is the same as ours; 2) the moon-year which is the revolutions of the moon about our parent body for the space of a year; 3) the tropical year which is the swing of the sun between Capricorn and Cancer; 4) the Venus Calendar. For this reason, we have found it relatively easy to read the dates of historical stones or steles, but since we cannot as yet decipher Mayan writing, we have no idea what happened on those dates.

The Venus Calendar is an excellent tool for computation. Venus, circling the sun on an inside orbit, makes thirteen revolutions to eight of the earth. Therefore in eight thirteens the two planets are back in the starting position. This is called the Full Cycle (104 years). Most American nations used the Half-Cycle of fifty-two years. There was also a Grand-Cycle of over three thousand years. When however both Full and Half cycles were ceremoniously tied, if the name was not specified, there could be confusion as to which was meant.

If this is the stone which Kate-Zahl ordered fashioned by his artisans, then as one enters the Museum down by the Zocalo, and looks along the passageway, the giant Calendar stone takes up almost the entire wall and dominates all of the visitor's perspective.

It is interesting also to speculate upon the other giant

block of basalt, the Altar of Sacrifices. It is exquisitely carved and polished. The present writer saw this master-piece in the company of Dr. A. Espejo and two other Mexican archeologists. "We know today that this is not Aztec. See the crude hatchet marks which cut through the carving to make the 'blood channel'? No, this too is Toltec. The Aztecs merely used it for their own purposes. Its true meaning is as lost to us today as it was to the Aztecs."

"But those other scars along some of the baseline?"

"Those were made by Spanish axes which it broke and shattered until they gave up trying to smash it. This too we inherit from the Toltec Empire."

THE ANTIQUITY OF TEOTIHUACAN

Since the time of carbon-dating, all dates on the ruins of the Ancients have been moved back from a thousand to fifteen hundred years. This brings Teotihuacan within the range of Tula.

What a shame we spend so much money in the near-east when here in the Americas, unexcavated (except by the spades of children who dig for trinkets to sell the tourists), is one of the earth's most fascinating cities - the probable ruins of Ancient Tula!

THE USE OF TILE

Tile was first discovered in the Pre-Incan ruins of Chan-Chan in South America. Pottery of great excellence was also found in this early City-State, as well as the first probable Great-Wall running around the land and the first massive works of irrigation, and the conduits bringing mountain water hundreds of miles to the city.

There is a possibility that the Pre-Incan ruins of the Andes are even older and their use of irrigation more extensive. This argument awaits the spade of the future archaeologist.

Chan-Chan had the world's greatest metal smiths. Even plating was common, and their work compares favorably with the finest done today. It is possible that this city was a contemporary of Tula. As yet, we do not know.

This city and many others had sunken baths and sewers.

The art of building these may have been lost about the time of the Chichimec invasions from the north about the Seventh Century A.D.

EMBROIDERY

According to Dr. A. Espejo of Mexico University, well known Mexican Archaeologist, the art of embroidery was very wide-spread in the Americas from the very earliest times. An Aztec maiden was not judged for her beauty as much as for her ability to embroider her husband's clothes.

THE ART OF DINING

It is very probable that much of our art of dining was brought across the seas from American conquests. See Bernal Diaz in his description of the table of Montezuma which he saw when he came into the city of Tenoch-titlan, Mexico with Cortez. Cloth tablecloths and napkins, finger bowls, tables and chairs and many other facts of modern living which we take for granted are described here with an air of amazement by the old soldier.

BUILDING MATERIALS

Stucco was widely used in the Americas with the finish of whitewash. Cut stone, cement and wood were also used, according to availability and location. In Chan-Chan, South America, finally overthrown by the rising Incan rulers of the Andes, most of the building was done with stucco, and porches were fastened to twined and trained fruit trees.

Chan-Chan was also famous for its factories, turning out cloth goods for export; possibly a world first in this line. Some sketches of these have been found on pottery.

HIGHWAYS

The great jungle-covered highways of Central America have been partially uncovered in spots to see how they were constructed. It was discovered that a nine-foot flagging of red sandstone blocks six to eight inches thick was laid down first, making the base for the hundred-foot-wide highways. This was then covered with a heavy layer of cement much stronger than we use today in modern highway building.

In South America narrower highways ran for thousands of miles, crossing vast gorges with swinging bridges, and using tunnels to cross other almost impassible ranges. At appropriate places along these were Inns for the travelers.

AMERICAN INDIAN DANCING

To the uninformed, American Indian dancing is jumping around and yelling. Between this point of view and that of E. Zimbalist there is a vast difference. The latter, a trained musician, makes the statement that Indian music is the most complicated in the world with its half and quarter tones and complicated changing rhythms.

For those who would like to see authentic dancing, there are two locations. In Gallup, New Mexico every August between the dates of 13 and 16 whichever one takes in a weekend, is the best. The Chamber of Commerce of Gallup pays the railroad expenses of dancers and furnishes their food while in Gallup. They sleep on the Indian campground. There are usually thirty-six tribes attending the festival from as far away as the Dakotas. (The Sioux are particularly colorful with their almost priceless ancient costumes of white beaded buckskin and the long eagle feather headdress of the Full-Chief.) The other location is Flagstaff, Arizona on the fourth of July. They have a similar arrangement.

The dances are very different as one who attends a festival will see. The plains tribes do the wildest types which are true because the pow-wow dancers are usually imitating the victory dance after a war-party-return. Each man is describing his own exploits to the rhythm and chanting. The Pueblos do the best group dancing. The concerted and complicated rhythms done by some twenty-six men in perfect synchronization is unequalled. The women are often pregnant, as that is the fertility symbol, and most dances are either prayers for rain, abundant crops, a prayer to the spirit of hunted animals before a hunt, or thanksgiving dances. These Pueblo dances are very ancient, running from our Pueblos to the center of Mexico, and undoubtedly, as Mexican scientists now believe, stem from Tollan probably long before the advent of the Prophet. It is the personal opinion of the present writer that they are older than that, since they seem to run down the Atlantic into South America, in a mere garbled form. They usually have two clowns and are often masked dances. They have a leader who directs them. The line of Katchinas approaching in the Hopi Pueblo is indeed impressive. (By the way, to digress for a moment, the ancient legend is that the Katchinas are from outer space and they visited the Pueblos once very long ago in a great silver sky ship which landed on the nearby Francisco Peaks, bearing gifts and dancing for the people.) The most graceful of all dances is the lovely Eagle Dance, while the hoop-dance showing great skill on the part of the solo dancer is usually a wedding dance.

The Navaho also have a group dance in the Yeibetchi. The weird high-pitched chanting in half and quarter tones is like something out of this world. The most amazing dance is the Navaho Fire-Dance. Many-Goats, their most famous fire-dancer, now gone to the Land of Shadows, lent the dance real grace and beauty as he dusted his too-thin body with sparks of living fire. (Do not get too close to this dance, which is too often done, as it is the final dance at Gallup. It could blind you.)

The humorous dances are delightful. The plains tribes do a charming Crow Dance, usually performed by children. One child comes out as the lead crow. He has a watermelon, and the others, dressed as a flock of crows, give him chase. The horse-tail dance is equally amusing. Men dressed with a long horse-tail attached to their bodies imitate horses in a herd with very funny results. The keenest Indian humor is shown by the clowns. Seldom is the performance repeated. One may make violent love to a very fat woman, or imitate Americans in shorts snapping cameras. Once a preacher came out with a dictionary for a bible and began to lecture an audience. The sleepier the audience became the louder he harangued them. The funniest dance the present writer ever saw was at Oraibi, the Hopi reservation in Arizona, when the clowns, representing Santa Claus and one of his helpers, gave a thin man a very large corset and a child a can of oil, and other inappropriate gifts.

The one with the greatest antiquity of all the dances, and to the present writer, the most intriguing, is the Crown-Dance of the Apaches. This is a millenia-old story of migrations which the tribe has combined with a puberty rite for young girls coming of age, or entering womanhood. This combination was necessary because, the Apaches tell me, the United States government would only allow them to keep one dance. It is often called the Devil Dance by enemies, which is an insulting term. Archaeologists should first read the Egyptian Book of the Dead before seeing this one. They will be amazed.

These are a few samples of rites which are among the most ancient on earth, being performed in our twentieth century.

HINTS TO TOURISTS

It is always well to ask the Indian's permission before snapping a picture. A gratituous tip of fifteen cents or a quarter is then usual. These are very poor people, and money is seriously important, often being food for the children.

Using a smile and a friendly attitude will often win permission for pictures, and if the tourist is not an American, then often a statement that one lives across the ocean will bring a more friendly attitude than is accorded to Americans. Unfortunately past and present injuries are too often keenly remembered when the Red Man meets an American, even if the American in question is innocent and uninformed.

248

Bibliography

AMERICAN INDIAN ART.
Written by a number of authorities. Illustrated by Indian artists. American Indian Tribal Arts Inc., 578 Madison Ave., New York, N.Y.

AMERICAN ANTIQUITY.
Society of American Archaeologists. University of Utah, Salt Lake City, Utah.

ANCIENT MEXICO.
An Introduction to Pre-Hispanic Cultures. The Allen Press, London, England.

THE ANTILLIAN CONTACTS OF INDIANS NORTH OF MEXICAN GULF.
International Congress of Americanists, Rio De Janeiro, Brazil. 1922.

ANTILLIAN CULTURE - ITS NORTH AND SOUTH AFFILIATIONS.
American Antillian Association, Copy 35. 1927.

THE ANDES.
Origin Y Desarrello de las Civilizations de Prehistoricas Andinas. Reimpreso de las Actes del 10, 11 Congress Americas de 1939. Lima, Peru. 1942. Edited by J.C. Tello, Curator, Lima Museum.

BANCROFT, HUBERT H.
Five Volumes of Antiquities, Native Races, etc. D. Appleton Co., 1875. (Very hard to obtain)
This is a mine of information because of quotations from ancient books now lost, and authors impossible to obtain. A must for Americanists of Pre-Hispanic Antiquity interests.

BANCROFT, HUBERT H.
History of Arizona and New Mexico from 1530. San Francisco Historical Society. 1874. (Out of Print.)

BANDELIER, ADOLFE.
The Delightmakers. (Indian dancing) Dodd Mead Inc. NY 1926.

BALDWIN, J.D.
Commentaries of Ancient America. Harper Bros. 1871.

BEALS, CARLTON.
Fire on the Andes. 1934. Mexican Maze. 1931. J.B. Lippencott, London, Philadelphia.

BELL, ROBERT E.
Trade Materials at Spiro Mound. 1947. American Antiquity, Vol. XII, No. 3, pp. 181-184. Dan Base Collection of Projectile Points of West Central Oklahoma. 1954. Oklahoma Anthropological Society, Bulletin 11. Pottery Vessels from Spiro Mound. 1953. Oklahoma Anthropological Society, Bulletin 1.

BELL, ROBERT E. AND BAERREIS, DAVID A.
A Survey of Oklahoma Archaeology. Texas Archaeological and Paleontological Society, Bulletin 22. 1951.

BRASSEUR DE BOURBOURG.

Studies in Mayan script. Translation of Troyane Mayan Anc. book. Archaeological Studies. History of Ancient Civilizations. Sur de Voyage Isthmus Tehuant-pec. Paris. 1861-64. Now out of print and almost impossible to obtain.

(It has been popular among scientists to be skeptical of this brilliant Frenchman of the last century. However, since he spoke Mayan fluently and had access to manuscripts of the Ancients now lost or hidden, it would seem to the present writer that this is a very short-sighted attitude. Many of the Histories which he quotes that have since been entirely lost made him an important source of information for Bancroft, who followed him a decade later.)

BURNETT, E.K. AND CLEMENTS, F.E.

The Spiro Mound. 1945. The Museum of Natural History, Heye Foundation, New York City.

BUNZEL, RUTH.

Zuni Ritualistic Poetry. Bureau of American Ethnology, 47 Wash. DC Government Printing Office, Washington 47, D.C.

CHATEAUBRIAND.

Sur le Voyage de. University of California Press.

This account of the early explorers up the Mississippi speaks of the long-boats of the Trading Indians met on the river.

COLLIER, JOHN.

The Indians of the Americas. 1947. W.W. Norton Co., New York, N.Y.

COOLIDGE, DANA.

The Last of the Seri.

CUSHING, FRANK H.

My Adventures in Zuni. Santa Fe Perapatetic Press. New Mexico. 1941. Zuni Creation Myths. U.S. Bureau. American Ethnological Annual Report, Vol. 13.

CORNYN, J.H.

Translator "Song Of Quetzalcoatl". Mexico University. (On reservation).

DALE, EDWARD E.

Indians of the Southwestern United States. 1954. St. Michael's Press, Arizona.

DECOODAH, LAST HIGH-PRIEST OF EXTINCT ELKS - TRADITIONS. 1847.

Translated and edited by Walter Pidgeon. Sampson Low and Son, 47 Kudgate Hill, London, England. 1853.

This red covered, gold embossed book is a complete amazement to the scientists who are able to see a copy. Now almost impossible to obtain, it should be reprinted by Oxford, Cambridge or some University of equal standing in the interest of the advancement of learning. The dates given by Decoodah for the Invasions of the Southerners - the Serpents led by the Tortoise - gives the best explanation of the language map which we have, and is interestingly substantiated by the carbon-dating of the first change of culture and the final overthrow and abandonment of these enormous man-made "Crests".

Young Pidgeon, a Caucasian surveyor who became intrigued by the Mounds being torn down by farmers, and with only a gun to obtain meat, a blanket to roll up in at night and his instruments, set out into what was wild woodland west of St. Louis to map "The Ancient Earthworks". One day he realized that he had an interested spectator - a tall dignified Indian garbed in a beautiful costume. By means of signs the stranger invited him to dinner and guided him to an Indian camp. There, after he had eaten many interesting foods, he was asked through an interpreter why he was mapping the "Crests" while his people were so busy destroying them? He answered simply: "Because I wish to bridge The Century of The Destroyers."

From this time on, his host, who was Decoodah, the last honored High-priest of an extinct nation, and keeper of the histories or chants, accompanied him, leading him to the most interesting Mounds, explaining the parts which rivers and streams had eroded away through the centuries, and marking out for him the missing part. Pidgeon became more and more amazed at this man's knowledge, trying desperately to learn enough Algonkin to better communicate.

Then after four months Decoodah announced that he wished to adopt Pidgeon as his son and thus pass on the Traditions which he had intended to carry to the grave when he had lost his own sons in the Black Hawk War. Thus he wished also to bridge The Century of The Destroyers. The rest of the book is filled with this history and how to read the Mounds.

Of this book, Dr. Clarke Wissler, of the Heye Foundation, New York City, wrote to the present writer: "We would be most honored to reprint this valuable book. However, please do not trust it to the mails. I will make a special trip to the West Coast next year personally to pick it up, and thank you so much for the privilege."

Unfortunately Dr. Wissler's death interfered with his plans.

DOCUMENTOS INEDITES RELACIENES DE YUCATAN IN PRIVATE COLLECTION MEXICO CITY,

quoted by Bancroft, is an amazing list of Christian terms and practices used by the Prophet, such as sin, Trinity, Virgin-birth of the Prophet, baptismal, marriage, confession when desired, etc. - a host of very Biblical practices.

DRIVER, HAROLD EDSON.
Indians of North America. University of Chicago Press. 1961.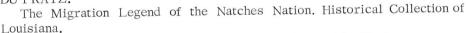

DU PRATZ.
The Migration Legend of the Natches Nation. Historical Collection of Louisiana.

This fascinating story of a nation which, along with allied groups were forced to abandon their cities on islands in the Southern Sea, due to the Civil War, and take to the mountains, finally coming north up the Mississippi in a huge migration movement of four waves, once more underwrites both Decoodah and the Language Map, as well as recent carbon-dating. On the Language Map, Wissler notes that many authorities find a relationship between Siouan (near the Dakotas), Iroquoian (on the Eastern Seaboard), Caddoan (Central Mississippi Basin) and Muskegean (Southern Msississippi), of whom the Natchez tribe was a member. The Natchez are now extinct.

FAWCETT, BRIAN.
Ruins in the Sky. 1958. Hutchison, London, England.

This is a hunt by young Fawcett for his father who disappeared in the South American Jungles while seeking a lost civilization. Although he did not succeed in his quest, he had some interesting experiences.

FERGUSON, ERNA.
Dancing Gods. (Discussion of the Ceremonials) University of New Mexico Press, Albuquerque, New Mexico. 1959.

FEWKES, JESSE WALTER.
Designs on Prehistoric Hopi Pottery. Bureau of Ethnology, Washington,

D.C. Report. 1911-12. Prehistoric Villages, Castles and Towers. Colorado Bureau of Ethnology, 1919. The Tusayan Katchinas. United States Bureau of Ethnology. Annual Volume 15.

FUNDABURK, E.L. AND FOREMAN, M.D.F.

Sun Circles and Human Hands. Laverne, Alabama. 1957.

GLADWIN, H.S.

The Chaco Branch Excavation of White Mound in Red Mesa Valley. Globe Arizona Press. 1945.

GRIFFIN, JAMES.

Archaeology of the Eastern United States. University of Chicago Press, Chicago, Illinois.

GOWER, C.D.

North and South Affiliations of Antillean Culture. American Archaeology and Anthropology Association Memo No. 35. 1927.

HAMILTON, HENRY W.

The Spiro Mound. The Missouri Archaeologist, Vol. 14. 1952.

HAINES, FRANCIS.

The Nez Perce. University of Oklahoma Press. 1955.

HARDIN, MADGE.

Early Days and Indian Ways. Western Lore Press.

HANNUM, ALBERTA.

Paint The Wind and Spin a Silver Dollar. Viking Press, New York, N.Y. 1958.

HARRINGTON, JOHN P.

Ethnogeography of the Tewa Indians. United States Bureau of American Ethnology Report, Washington, D.C. 1916.

HEWITT, EDGAR LEE.

Ancient Life in the American Southwest. Bobbs Merrill Co., Indianapolis, Indiana. 1930. Ancient Andean Life and Indian Cultures. Tudor Publishing Co., New York, N.Y. 1943. Chaco Canyon and Its Monuments. University of New Mexico Press. 1936.

HUNTINGTON, ELLSWORTH.

The Red Man's Continent. Yale University Press. 1920.

ILIFF, FLORA GREGG.

People of the Blue Water (The Havasupai). Harper Bros, New York, N.Y. 1957.

This is a human interest story of a young Caucasian school teacher from the east who fell in love with a brave and married within the tribe.

JIMENEZ, MARCOS.

Relaciones Geograficas de Indes de Peru, 1881-97. Author in La Espada, Madrid. (On reserve, University of Mexico.)

JENES, DAVID.

Forty Years Among The Indians. Western Lore Press.

JUARRES.

History of Guatemala. (Very Important for its Fuentes History now lost. Quoted by Bancroft. On Reserve, University of Mexico.)

KROEBER.

Coast and Highlands of Prehistoric Peru. American Anthropologist, 1929.

LORD KINGSBOROUGH.

Mexican Antiquities. Now almost unobtainable. Other books now lost. Quoted at length by Bancroft. Some student should do a biography of this gentle son of the English aristocracy of the last century who was so fascinated by

252

the magnetic Figure of the Pale God that he mortgaged all of his holdings and died miserably in a debtor's prison. He still is the world authority on the Prophet. However, I have been unable to obtain any of his books. There must be a great deal of valuable knowledge of the First Century of the Americas in some shelf of old books, and of the tremendous Personality who dominated those yellowed pages.

LA CASAS.

Historia Apologetica. Now lost. Historia General de Las Casas de Nueve Espana. Vol. 5, University of Mexico. 1938. On Reserve.

This saintly monk who walked the Americas during the terrible times of the Conquest has an invaluable collection of facts and stories on the Prophet according to Bancroft, who evidently saw the book now lost, quoting from it widely.

LAMB, DANA AND GINGER.

Quest for the Lost Mayan City. Harper Bros., New York, N.Y. 1955.

LEIGH, RANDOLPH.

Forgotten Waters. J.B. Lippincott, London, New York, Philadelphia.

LUMMIS, CHARLES F.

Pueblo Indian Folk Stories. The Tewa, Taos and Isleta Pueblos. The Century Co., New York. First published in 1891.

MAYA AND THEIR NEIGHBORS, THE.

AAAS Symposium, 1940.

MARKHAM, CLEMENTS.

The Inca of Peru. 1910, London. Reprinted by Lima Museum.

This scientist made the statement that after studying the Incan Civilization for two years he thought he knew everything about it, but after fifty years decided that he knew nothing.

MARRIOTT, ALICE.

These Are The People. Indians of the Four Corners. Thos. Cowell Publishing Co., New York, N.Y. 1952.

MATHEWS, JOHN LOS.

The Osage. (A Siouan-speaking Oklahoma Tribe) The University of Oklahoma Press, Norman, Oklahoma. 1932.

Story of an Indian Agent on a Reservation. The Great-Spirit has Prophet's South American name.

MORLEY, SYLVANNUS G.

The Ancient Maya. 1947. Oxford University Press, England, University of California, Berkeley, California. Used as a text by the University of Mexico.

NATIONAL GEOGRAPHIC MAGAZINE.

Staircase Farms of the Ancients. Pre-Incan Farming and Transportation. 1913.

NATIONAL GEOGRAPHIC MAGAZINE.

January 1959. Article - Dzibilchaltun, (Lost City of the Maya) by E. Wyllys Andrews of Tulane University.

ORR, KENNETH G.

Field Report on the Excavation of Indian Villages in Vicinity of Spiro Mound. Oklahoma Prehistorian, Vol. 2. 1939. The Archaeological Situation at Spiro. American Antiquity, Vol. 11, No. 4. 1946. Survey of Caddoan Area Archaeology. Archaeology of Eastern United States, by Jas Griffin.

PARSONS, ELSIE CLEWS,

Pueblo Indian Religion. University of Oklahoma Press. 1939. (2 Vols.) Winter and Summer Dances at Zuni. American Archaeology and Ethnology

Series, University of California Press. Vol. 13.

PECK, ANN MERRIMAN.

The Pageant of South American History. Longman Green Co., London, New York. 1941. The Pageant of Mid-American History. Longman Green, London, New York, Canada. 1947.

PRESCOTT, WM. W.

Conquest of Peru. Thos. Crowell Publishing Co., New York, N.Y. 1947. A Classical Study.

PRIESTLEY, J.B. AND JACQUETTE.

Journey Down a Rainbow. Harper Bros., New York, N.Y. 1955. Indian Dancing.

POSNANSKY, A.

Prehistoric Monuments of Peru. Privately Printed by the Author in Lima University Press. Magnificently illustrated. Price $25.00.

It has been popular to laugh at this scientist because he believes that the ancient conduits bringing water from the Pleistocene Glaciers were of that age. He just may be right.

REGAL, ALBERTO.

The Roads of the Incas in Peru. University of Peru in Lima Collection. 1936.

RIVET, P.

L'Orfevrerie Pre-Columbienne des Antilles. Journal Society of Americanists, Paris.

ROGERS, DAVID BANKS.

Prehistoric Man on the Santa Barbara Coast. Santa Barbara Museum. About 1941. Dr. Rogers was curator of the Museum at this time.

This friend of the present writer explained the impression of a 100-ft. plank ship caulked with tar found some forty feet under the beach on one of the Islands with implements suggesting the site was a dry-dock repair point for the Ancients. The wood had entirely rotted away.

ROSS, PATRICIA FENT.

Made in Mexico. New York, N.Y. Alfred A. Knopf, New York, N.Y. 1955.

This red-haired woman went to Mexico for a three weeks vacation and never left. Now a citizen of the country, she speaks all of the Indian tongues and travels alone and unarmed among the wild tribes where no soldier or Spanish speaking Mexican would dare to go. Her lectures at the University of Mexico are filled with fascinating experiences and adventures. However, her opinion of the Prophet is entirely Aztec in viewpoint.

ROWE, JOHN H.

Introduction to Archaeology of Cuzco, South America. Peabody Museum and American Archaeological Study of Harvard University. Vol. 27 - No. 2.

SAHAGUN, FRAY BERNARDIND DE.

On reserve, University of Mexico. (Spanish) History. Works of the Sansen D'Abbeville. 1667. L'Amerique (French) Block and Co., Cleveland, Ohio. 1959.

As the Geographer to Louis 14th of France, this Frenchman travels to Quivira among other ancient cities. He describes the customs of Indians not yet crushed by the weight of the Conquest. The domesticated mountain sheep and buffalo interest him as well as the materials used for clothing. For example he mentions the (new wild) American flax.

SANDEZ, MARIE.

Crazy-Horse, War-Chief of the Sioux. 1942. Cheyenne Autumn. 1953. McGraw Hill, London, Toronto, United States.

SARMIENTES.

Relaciones. (Spanish mss.) Reserve University of Mexico. Was in Kingsborough Collection. Now Lost.

SPINDEN, HERBERT J.

Ancient Civilizations of Mexico and Central America. Heye Foundation, Museum of Natural History, New York, N.Y. 1928. Indians of North America. University of Chicago Press. 1961.

SQUIER, GEORGE E.

Peru, Land of the Incas. (Very hard to obtain) London, 1877. Now long out of print.

This book was quoted profusely by Bancroft describing the travels of George Squier, and from this source comes the description of the Incan ruins at the Lake of Vira Cocha and the then standing statue of the Prophet.

SQUIER, E.Q.

American Archaeological Researches. London, Now probably lost. Quoted by Bancroft.

SWAN, MICHAEL.

Temples of the Sun and Moon. (Delightful Travel) Jonathan Cape, London. 1954.

SQUIER, E.L.

Tanama, The Trembling God. (Earthquake) also Children of the Twilight. Cosmopolitan Book Corp., New York, N.Y. 1926.

TELLO, J.C.

(See Andes under A) This brilliant scientist, curator of the Lima Museum to the time of his death, did much to uncover the lost history of his people - the Quichua Indians of the Incan Empire.

TODD, MILLICENT.

Peru: a Land of Contrasts. Little Brown, New York, N.Y. 1918.

TORQUEMADA.

An important historian of Mexico. Works now lost are quoted by Bancroft.

TRIBBLES, THOMAS H.

Buckskin Blanket Days. Written 1905. Doubleday, New York, N.Y.

TROWBRIDGE, H.M.

Analysis of Spiro Mound Textiles. American Antiquity, Facts and Comment, Vol. 4. 1938.

UNDERHILL, RUTH.

Red Man's America. University of Cambridge London Press, University of Chicago. 1953.

VEGA, GARCILASSE DE LA.

Commentaries. (Now Lost) Quoted extensively by Bancroft. One copy Mexican Reserve (Private Collection)

VERRILL, A. HYATT.

Old Civilizations of the New World. Bobbs Merrill, Indianapolis, Indiana. 1929. On reading lists of Redlands University in Archaeology.

VERRILL, A. HYATT AND RUTH.

American Ancient Civilizations. G.P. Putnam, New York, N.Y.

VELASCO, LOPEZ DE.

Geography and Descriptions of Indian Lands in the Years. 1571-74. Justo Zamora, Madrid. 1894.

VESTAL, STANLEY.

War Path and Council Fire. Random House, New York, N.Y. 1948.

VON HAGEN, VICTOR.

The Highway of the Sun - Machu Pichu. Duell Sloan and Pearce, New York, N.Y. Little Brown, Toronto, Boston. 1955.

WECKLER, J.E. JR.

Polynesians, Explorers of the Pacific. Smithsonian No. 3704 Jan. 1942, Washington D.C.

WHITNEY, CHARLES FREDRICK.

Indian Designs and Symbols. Newcomb and Gauss, Salem, Mass. 1925.

WHITE, SARAH.

Human Effigy Pipes from the Spiro Mound. Oklahoma Prehistorian. Vol. 3, No. 1. 1940.

WISSLER, CLARKE.

The Indian Cavalcade. Sheridan House, New York, N.Y. Indians of the U.S. Heye Foundation, New York, N.Y. Social Life of the Blackfoot. American Museum of Natural History Press, New York, N.Y. Anthropological Papers and North American Indians of the Plains. Heye Foundation, New York, N.Y. 1932.

WRIGHT, H.B.

Aw-aw-Tam and Indian Story Tellers. Legends of the Pagago. Long-Age-Told.

XIMENEZ.

History of the Kings of the Qui-Chi. Now lost. Quoted by Bancroft.

CARBON DATING. 1961.

Radio carbon dates from Archaeological sites in Oklahoma.

BELL, ROBT. E.

Anthropological Society, University of Oklahoma.

The dates on the Spiro Mound run on the average as dated by the Laboratories of the University of Michigan 2286 years ago plus or minus 200 years.

Three dates are given by three different laboratories. M is that of Michigan, O is that of the Exploration Department and Geochemical Laboratory, Humble Oil Co., Houston, Texas and R is that of the Institute of Nuclear Sciences, Scientific and Industrial Research, Lower Butt, New Zealand.

The dates run from some time before the Christian Era (500 yrs.) to almost recent, where recent material has fallen into, or spread into crevasses. However on the whole the dates of Decoodah as from 400 to 700 AD for the first Serpent Invasions and 1000 AD as total abandonment is amazingly borne out by carbon dating.

The good Lightning.